INTRODUCTION

When we think about influence, we also think about power and authority. We consider it more traditionally: leaders' influence on their followers or parents' influence on their children. However, influence exists in more than one dynamic. It shapes the whole world and affects how we interact with and think of people—and vice versa. Influence is about connecting with people and tapping into the innate desire for belonging and connection. It often determines our first impression of others and how much we get out of a new relationship, making it a valuable tool in dealing with strangers. Despite how normal and natural influence is, it is a powerful tool, and if misused or used by the wrong people, it can have dangerous consequences. We see this in cult dynamics and even in the dynamic between teenagers and their peers, often referred to as manipulation and peer pressure. Learning about human psychology is necessary to wield that kind of power—and to wield it responsibly. This book will divide these 21 psychology laws based on their role in helping you build your influence.

In Part 1, we explore laws that can help us form connections with the people we want to influence. The familiarity and halo effect show us how to find mutual ground and become someone people want to connect with. The reciprocity principle touches on the human need to return a favor and how you can leverage that to connect with strangers. Through mirroring, we learn how to mimic people's behavior to create a comfortable environment for strangers to communicate with us. As we wrap up this section, we will learn about the power of names and how they might be the most under recognized tool when it comes to forging connections.

In Part 2, we discuss cultivating trust. True influence comes from people's confidence in you. If they believe that you are reliable, they will be inclined to listen to you. We will learn about the power of vulnerability and how to use it to build trust. The consistency bias is another tool we will explore in the context of trust-building. If you prove yourself reliable once or twice, people will begin to assume they can rely on you in any situation. We also explore how contagious moods and emotions are and how to use that to exert influence. The primacy effect is the real star of this segment because it deals with the power and importance of first impressions and how to create and use a good first impression.

In Part 3, we delve into actually sparking influence. The social proof theory is one of the leading theories in this area. But what does it mean, and how do you use it? We learn all of that here. We also discover how much scarcity affects people's decisions and how you can use it ethically to influence them. The anchoring and framing effect takes us back to the primacy effect, and we see how marketing teams use this to guide people's spending.

Part 4 is all about driving action with the influence you have gained. The foot-in-the-door technique teaches us how to leverage our influence and not take no for an answer. We learn why people might hesitate to act or change with the loss aversion principle. The authority effect teaches us to position ourselves as authority

How To Influence STRANGERS

21 Timeless Laws of Human Psychology and How to Use Them Today

ALBION BURNS

CONTENTS

figures to overcome this hesitation. Even Jesus used stories in his teachings—he used them to impart his wisdom to his followers—and we learn how to do that with the power of storytelling. Finally, we explore the delicate yet important balance between emotions and logic.

Let's dive in!

PART I:

BUILDING CONNECTION

LAW 1:

THE FAMILIARITY EFFECT

People often seek solace in familiar things. They are drawn to buildings resembling their homes and people who speak like them. This psychological principle is known as the familiarity effect. It explains why people are more likely to trust and engage with individuals they have encountered before. We order food from the same restaurant and get the same dish each time. When we go home from work, we take the same route and even stick to the same fashion style. We crave the familiar. However, as someone looking to impact a stranger's life, this can be a stumbling block. How do you get close to someone if they won't try something or someone new? In this chapter, we will explore the science behind the familiarity effect and its role in influencing others, particularly strangers. You will learn how to turn this obstacle into a propellant.

This chapter delves into the science behind this effect, examines its influence on others, and provides practical strategies for creating familiarity with strangers.

Why People Trust What They Recognize

In the 1960s, psychologist Robert Zajonc highlighted a key scientific fact: repeatedly exposing the human brain to a stimulus increases the likelihood of developing positive feelings toward it. His experiments demonstrated that familiarity doesn't require something tangible, such as people or food, to evoke positive attachment. He showed participants abstract shapes and nonsense words and noticed that, despite their lack of meaning, participants rated them favorably due to repeated exposure.

What does this mean? It means that our yearning for the familiar is not a conscious trait. It is a subconscious phenomenon that shapes our preferences before we think about them logically. The restaurant you swear makes the best pizzas might be average, but it seems even better because it is familiar.

Researchers believe this desire for familiarity developed as a survival mechanism. Early humans needed to distinguish between safe and unsafe environments, associating safety with what was known and avoiding the unknown as potentially dangerous. The saying, "The devil you know is better than the angel you don't," stems from this predisposition. Over time, this tendency to equate safety with familiarity became deeply ingrained in our psychology.

Studies have found that when exposed to familiar stimuli, the brain activates reward pathways, particularly in the amygdala and prefrontal cortex. This activation creates a neurological and emotional sense of comfort and ease. Remarkably, this effect applies even when the object is seemingly unfamiliar. A mailbox you pass by daily may not stand out, but your brain still recognizes it as familiar. Familiarity is a powerful force in shaping human behavior.

Trust and familiarity are the building blocks of our relationships. We trust someone or something because we have known them for a long time. Babies trust their mothers because they have spent nine months growing inside them. You trust your partner because you know them well. You may always buy a particular brand of laundry detergent because you are familiar with it. We prefer the known because it reduces risk and creates a sense of safety.

This effect also explains why we are drawn to people who remind us of ourselves in social contexts. Psychologists call this implicit egotism—a bias toward anything associated with our identity. For example, people tend to favor others with similar names, home-towns, or interests—elements that create an immediate sense of familiarity.

Practical Strategies for Creating Familiarity with Strangers

It sounds daunting, but you can use this to your advantage, especially when interacting with strangers. Now that you understand how this works, I will outline six practical and effective steps for familiarizing yourself with people you have just met.

1. **Find and Highlight Common Ground:**

   As I mentioned, we are subconsciously drawn to people with whom we share experiences, values, or interests. Can you think about how you met your best friend? Many people meet the closest and most valuable connections through a random conversation. For example, if you see someone at an art gallery, you can ask them what they like about the piece they're looking at or which one is their favorite. Most people want to share anyway and just need a push. Your question can be that push. The information they reveal might help you find common ground and strengthen your friendship. You may discover that you like the same artist or art style—a connection is formed just like that.

2. **Use Subtle Repetition:**

For instance, if you are networking at an event, repeating your name at the beginning and end of a conversation makes it more likely that the other person will remember you. Gently echoing a stranger's words (a technique known as mirroring, which we will explore in later chapters) can make them feel understood and comfortable. These are emotions associated with familiarity.

3. **Leverage Digital Channels**

Social media is your go-to if the strangers you're trying to impact are on the internet. The world is now a globally digital village. Everybody knows everybody or knows someone who knows someone. If you engage with someone's posts consistently—maybe by commenting, liking, or sharing—you can forge a connection with them. If there's anything the digital age has helped us achieve, it is seamless connections—none of the awkwardness of real-life communication.

4. **Engage in Positive Interactions**

The quality of initial interactions matters greatly. Positive experiences amplify the familiarity effect, making future encounters more favorable. Whether through kindness, humor, or attentiveness, creating a memorable first impression increases the likelihood of being trusted and liked.

Familiarity builds gradually. Establishing trust with a stranger requires consistent effort and genuine engagement. Patience is key, as repeated exposure over time solidifies the sense of safety and reliability needed for trust to flourish.

Trying too hard to force a connection is a red flag. Picture it: if someone consistently tries to sell you a product, you become wary of it and start questioning their intentions. Your motives for attempting to forge a connection must be genuine or, at least, mutually beneficial. Why do you want to influence a stranger? Is it because you want to get something from them, or do you genuinely believe the two of you can create something extraordinary?

If there's anything to note, it is that the subconscious mind shapes so much of our behavior. If you understand this and how much it affects what people trust and connect to, then you can leverage it effectively. When we connect, they connect so profoundly because the interaction speaks to an emotion we hold dear or a familiar situation.

When you try to build this type of connection with strangers, you pave the way for something meaningful and beautiful to blossom. Nobody affects us as much as friends and family, with whom we have established connections. If we recreate this familiarity with strangers, we might have hacked the first and most crucial step of influencing people.

LAW 2:

THE HALO EFFECT

To humanity, perception is rarely objective. Instead, our biases color our opinions and perceptions; we form them daily without realizing it. One such bias, the Halo Effect, describes the phenomenon where a positive or negative impression of a person or entity influences how we evaluate their other qualities upon first glance.

Psychologist Edward Thorndike first identified this effect in 1920. In one of his research procedures, which he conducted within the military, he found that superior officers were likely to match traits like reliability and intelligence to concepts like attractiveness and physique. An assumed appearance of a person is an encouraging marker to superior officers. This marker increases the chances of a recruit being deemed "trustworthy." As such, the Halo Effect can be described as a subtle yet profound phenomenon emphasizing the importance of key elements such as appearance, tone, and presentation in shaping interactions. It is both a tool and a challenge—one that can elevate your personal and professional image or distort your understanding of someone else's image.

The Process of Understanding the Halo Effect

The Halo Effect operates on a simple yet powerful principle: our minds tend to generalize from limited information. A positive characteristic (such as physical attractiveness, confidence, or eloquence) can create a "halo" that biases our evaluation of unrelated attributes. For instance, well-dressed and articulate people are often assumed to be intelligent, trustworthy, and capable, even without concrete evidence to support these assumptions. An example of this is how we expected, when we were younger, that people in political or social positions of power, just by being in those positions, were qualified and correct in whatever they were doing.

This cognitive shortcut helps us navigate a complex social world but often leads to oversimplified and inaccurate judgments. A better understanding of the Halo Effect can significantly improve day-to-day interactions by helping individuals guard against shortcomings they didn't even know existed while enabling them to leverage the genuine qualities they possess. Being more approachable as a result of understanding this concept helps significantly in shaping how a stranger perceives you.

What Is It About the Power of Appearance, Tone, and Presentation?

As a concept that relies heavily on the dynamics created by lasting and memorable first impressions, the Halo Effect depends on factors like appearance, tone, and presentation to shape how someone is initially perceived. Edward Thorndike echoes this in his work. These elements act as powerful cues that influence how others evaluate the character, abilities, or intentions of a stranger or anyone encountered in daily life.

The first of these, physical attractiveness, is considered by researchers to be one of the most potent triggers of the Halo Effect (if not the most significant). Edward Thorndike's exploration showed that we often consider attractive individuals more competent, friendly, and destined for success, associating them with traits like reliability. But beyond good looks, grooming, attire, and posture also play significant roles. A well-dressed individual is more likely to command respect and attention due to having an "aura," irrespective of their qualifications.

The second concept, tone, reflects how we speak—our tone, pace, intonation, and even accent. These elements profoundly alter how others perceive us, either drawing them closer out of interest or pushing them away due to irritation, for example. A calm, confident, and warm tone can create a good impression, leading others to see us as competent and approachable. This approachability fosters comfort in interactions, especially with strangers. Conversely, a harsh or hesitant tone may undermine trust and credibility. For instance, children are more likely to be welcoming toward a friendly person, such as someone who rewards them for achievements, while shying away from someone perceived as threatening, like a person who yells at them.

Clear, concise, and engaging communication leaves a lasting impression, while disorganized or overly complex presentations can lead others to view us as less competent. For example, a person with a meticulously tailored outfit often receives compliments and positive attention in almost any setting. This admiration encourages interaction, as people are drawn to individuals who inspire them or represent qualities they admire. On the other hand, someone with a poorly assembled outfit might be ignored or avoided, even when discussed by those familiar with them. Humans have a tendency to emphasize socially acceptable and appreciated concepts, avoiding topics that could lower the energy of a room. It's much easier to tell someone how lovely they smell and ask for their perfume recommendation than to confront them about an unpleasant odor—a much more complicated conversation.

LAW 3:

THE RECIPROCITY PRINCIPLE

This book references the work of renowned psychologist Dr. Robert Cialdini. In this chapter, we will discuss one fundamental social and psychological fact he popularized in his book: reciprocity. During Christmas time, there are a lot of gift exchanges—Secret Santa at work and the gift swap under the Christmas tree. It is considered bad practice to come empty-handed when attending a wedding. Why? Well, because human beings are naturally wired to return favors. We can't shake off this psychological necessity, no matter how much we want to fight it. There are many theories about why humans behave this way. However, my favorite school of thought is that it restores balance. There is a "give-and-take" dynamic that helps restore balance when we draw resources from someone or somewhere. So, your small acts of kindness and generosity can open unexpected doors for you. Why should kindness be motivated solely by our inherent desire to do good? The reciprocity principle ensures that people who perform these small favors or acts of kindness can reap the fruits those seeds have planted.

A Universal Law of Human Behavior

Cialdini experimented with soda and a raffle ticket, proving that this isn't just an imaginary concept but a tangible one. He wanted to know what persuaded people to act and found that being on the receiving end of a kind action prompted them to try to return the favor. In his experiment, participants who were given an unsolicited bottle of soda were more likely to buy the raffle ticket the researchers were selling afterward. Because the researchers had shown these people an unprompted act of kindness, they felt the urge to reciprocate.

If a stranger holds a door open for you, you feel gratitude. You might say thank you and keep going. However, if you meet that same person at your favorite coffee shop a couple of hours later, you might feel obligated to buy their drink for them. You can use this principle in your daily interactions with strangers if you are trying to create influence. We evolved by leaning on each other, which is how our healthy society functions to this day. Once you understand this principle of human nature, everything becomes markedly easier.

These minor acts of thoughtfulness are the most rewarding. Why? Because people see them as genuine and a pleasant surprise. They might get suspicious or wary if you offer to pay off a stranger's car debt. However, if you help that same person carry a bunch of groceries to their car, they will be much more open to your help. In later chapters, we will discuss the primacy effect and first impressions. If you want to use the reciprocity principle to influence strangers, here is a how-to guide:

- **Start with Giving**: Begin every interaction by offering something of value. In the example I gave above when helping someone take groceries to their car, the value you're providing is your time and human resources. If you help pay for someone's coffee, you give them your hard-earned money. If you help a mom with a fussy baby at the park, give her a much-needed break. This is enough to spark a connection.

- **Be Authentic**: Sincerity is non-negotiable. I am sure you are also good at telling when someone's act of kindness comes from a place of exploitation. The hairs on the back of your neck stand, or you feel uncomfortable in your belly. Treat this act of giving as second nature. Otherwise, people will be wary of what you want and less likely to accept your help.

- **Balance Generosity with Discernment**: While generosity is powerful, it's essential to recognize its limits. If you give too much and overextend yourself, people will be willing to exploit you. More importantly, you can either start feeling burnt out or the value of your kindness will drop.

Reciprocation in Action

Imagine Francis, a Romanian student aiming for scholarships in Austria, attending a seminar on the course of his dreams. However, looking around the room, Francis spots someone around him struggling to find a seat. He is kind enough to offer him and takes to standing instead. From that action, there is an increased possibility of that generosity prompting a conversation between the two after that seminar, a reciprocated norm most would consider.

The value of such an action would be the possibilities that arise from such a random act of kindness. Socially speaking, depending on the individual receiving that action, a different message is sent: either friendly, with potential for romance, or socially appropriate, as is often the case with giving up seats for the elderly and physically impaired.

Similarly, this simple act of generosity could lead to a conversation, resulting in a drastically more productive outcome. Francis, who has dreams of a scholarship in Austria, through that act of kindness, could be interacting with someone with the ability to make an introduction to a professor or university official with scholarship insights. Here, Francis' decision to stand for a stranger—seemingly inconsequential at the moment—sets off a chain of events that could shape his academic journey. This is the Reciprocity Principle in motion: a modest gesture creating ripples of opportunity.

If you have ever studied a painting up close or even the formation of rocks, you will know by now that nothing is more substantial than little and deliberate acts of pressure. The small and consistent brushstrokes make the painting a masterpiece. Grand canyons are formed by small and consistent water pressure. Small and thoughtful acts of reciprocity can also impact people's lives significantly. In our next chapter, we will explore mirroring and how it works hand in hand with reciprocity to help you build influence.

LAW 4:

MIRRORING

To create a winning first impression, we must first know the type of people we hope to impress or build an impression on. Once this is established, we can adjust to fit into the best versions of ourselves to gain recognition. Mirroring takes this a step further. After establishing an impression, we have to maintain and improve it. One of the best ways to do this is by making subtle changes to our behavior, body language, speech patterns, and language use. We make these changes the more involved we become with our audience because we observe their behaviors to determine how best we can fit in with them. This subtle mimicking of behaviors is called 'mirroring.'

The law of mirroring is based on recognizing how mirror neurons, which are specialized cells in the brain, are responsible for identifying the actions you observe and replicating them. These neurons enable us to empathize with others because they create a sense of shared experience and understanding. Mirroring taps into the human need for social connection and belonging. It can generate a sense of similarity and harmony between people because we are wired to seek relationships and communities where we feel understood and valued. As a result, mirroring plays a significant role in social interactions, communication, and the development of trust while helping you build a bridge between yourself and others to make interactions smoother and more effective.

A 1999 study by Chartrand and Bargh found that participants who were subtly mimicked by a researcher reported feeling more positively about the interaction and were more likely to view the researcher as likable and trustworthy. This shows that mirroring can profoundly affect interpersonal relationships since it signals to others that they are understood and accepted. When you mirror their behavior, people are more likely to agree with or cooperate with you, especially in high-stakes situations like negotiations or conflict resolution. Let's get into it.

The Psychology of Mimicking Behavior to Build Rapport

You must have noticed how people adjust their speech patterns, tone, or even body language based on whom they speak with. If you're a manager, you've probably noted how language use changes when your teammates talk to you vs. when they speak amongst themselves. You may also have found yourself changing your mode of interaction when relating to people, especially those you want to convince or negotiate with. People often pick up cues from the person they're having a one-on-one interaction with and mirror those cues back to them without consciously realizing it. Mirroring has much to do with subtly mimicking people—their behavior, speech, or emotions—to gain their social acceptance and approval. As previously mentioned, this is the job of part of the brain's mirror neuron system. These neurons enable us to replicate the social cues we have observed after recognizing the difference between our behaviors and those in our environment. It is also a key ingredient for building empathy, which makes mirroring integral to building rapport.

Behaviors are not formed in a vacuum. As social creatures, we depend a lot on our nurturing to form the basis of our personalities. As a result, everyone resorts to mimicking behaviors to build rapport, seek connection, and find acceptance, especially in new situations or environments. Mirroring is the human, nonverbal way to tell the people around us that, even if we are new to them, we are similar to them and should not be regarded as a threat or with suspicion. Ironically, psychologists also refer to this as the chameleon effect. This chameleon effect reflects the human desire to mimic what we see or experience, similar to the way the chameleon changes its color. We do this in various ways, but it could be because we want to fit in or protect ourselves, like the chameleon.

Studies have consistently shown to a great degree how important mirroring is in promoting unity and rapport. Social psychology suggests that people are more likely to feel comfortable and open if they think the people around them are similar. Mirroring, as a technique, taps into this innate preference for similarity. Behavioral scientist Tanya Chartrand and social psychologist John Bargh engaged two groups of participants in an experiment to explore this part of the human psyche. They found that the group subtly mirrored by an experimenter liked and related more smoothly to the experimenter than those who weren't. Even when unconscious, mimicry is a cheat code to foster positive perceptions because people will often see themselves in a good light. If you are similar to them, they're likely to project their perception of goodness onto you.

From a psychological perspective, mirroring activates mirror neurons—specialized cells in the brain that become active when we do something and see someone else do the same thing. These neurons are central to empathy and social understanding, helping us interpret the intentions and emotions of others. Mirroring someone else creates a subtle neurological resonance in their mind. It acts like a special note to their subconscious that you see them. This results in a feeling of shared mutual understanding and emotional connection.

Mirroring also works exceptionally well in professional and high-stakes environments. Negotiators, therapists, and sales professionals use this technique as standard practice to create emotional connections with their clients. As a negotiator, you stand a better chance of getting the other party to be more receptive to your proposals if you align your tone and posture to develop a form of camaraderie. Similarly, therapists use mirroring to signal empathy and validation. It is the baseline for interacting with clients and getting them to open up more freely. However, in these situations, overly obvious mimicry can appear insincere and potentially backfire, damaging trust in a way you can't recover.

Genuine mirroring requires attentiveness, adaptability, and nuance. You should never rigidly copy someone's movements. Instead, mirroring should focus on attuning yourself to the energy and rhythm of the situation while responding in ways that naturally reflect their communication style. To do this successfully, you have to be highly observant. In this context, being observant means paying close attention to their body language, tone, and pacing so you can better understand their communication style.

Best of all, mirroring creates an environment that leaves everyone involved feeling confident and psychologically secure. In this state, people feel understood and valued because these slight adjustments significantly impact the person and the emotional connection of an interaction. Once you've learned how to apply it skillfully, it can become the best tool in your arsenal for bridging divides, fostering empathy, and nurturing relationships.

Subtle Ways to Apply Mirroring in Conversations

Because mimicking behavior works subconsciously, it is often imperceptible to the individuals involved. To take note of it and make it work to your advantage, you must consciously track what works and what doesn't. Here are some things you can take note of:

1. **Nonverbal Synchronization:**

   Mirroring a person's physical gestures, posture, and movement creates a persona they can see and relate to, thereby improving your interpersonal connection with them. People are more comfortable around those who feel familiar, and a simple, easy way to create that feeling is by reflecting their body language with yours. Find mirroring techniques that work with whoever you're speaking with to convey your subconscious agreement and engagement. Use this to create an environment that fosters a sense of safety, encouraging open dialogue. However, ensure you're keeping it subtle. I'll tell you a secret: match their general posture instead of trying to copy their every move. If they seem relaxed, match that. If they seem serious, don't counter it with a calm demeanor—mirror their seriousness instead.

2. **Linguistic Adaptation:**

This is already something everyone is familiar with. Mirroring should go beyond body language to how we talk. Pay attention to the pace, tone, and even the choice of words someone uses. If they speak slowly and thoughtfully, adjust your rhythm to align with theirs. If they're enthusiastic and animated, bring similar energy to your conversation. Matching someone's tone, tempo, and even choice of words reinforces the alignment that body language has built. A study in the *Journal of Personality and Social Psychology* showed that when you use your listener's language style while conversing with them, you improve the chances of finding common ground. Because this is a relatively easy way to establish trust and make your message more relatable and engaging, it is an essential aspect of mirroring. However, ensure that in mirroring, you are not masking—covering up the entirety of your personality to become a 'personality doppelganger' of your listener. Maintain your authenticity to avoid sounding like a hollow caricature.

3. **Emotional Resonance:**

Emotional mirroring is one of the most impactful ways to connect deeply with someone. When individuals mirror emotions, such as reflecting a smile or showing concern in response to distress, it triggers emotional validation. This type of mimicry signals empathy and understanding and is the first step to validating the feelings of others. A great way to practice this is by starting with friends and family. When they share a joyful story that you don't think is particularly exciting, attempt to show enthusiasm and mirror their excitement. If they're discussing a challenge with an evident solution, lead with empathy to show that you're attuned to their emotional state before offering your solution. Genuine emotional resonance is your best bet for making people feel seen and valued, creating room for trust and collaboration.

4. **Cultural and Contextual Sensitivity:**

You should never use mirroring as a one-size-fits-all technique. Cultural differences, personal boundaries, and social settings should determine how you put it into practice. The benefits of mirroring are great, but its application should be based on the nuances of your situation or environment. Cultural norms and individual preferences affect how mirroring is perceived. More often than not, overt mimicry will alienate your audience. However, sometimes, people expect you to respond to their interactions with similar energy levels. In professional settings, subtle, almost imperceptible adjustments tailored to the situation are more likely to succeed.

5. **Practice Active Listening:**

Mirroring starts with paying attention. Active listening is a special part of mirroring because it emphasizes a conversation's verbal and conversational aspects. Without it, effective mirroring is nearly impossible. Active listening significantly improves how effective you'll be at mirroring by providing context for the appropriate cues to mimic. By actively listening, you'll better grasp the energy, phrasing, and emotions you need to mirror for effective interactions. One way to show you're actively listening is to maintain eye contact, demonstrating that they have your full attention. Active listening must be genuine to be effective.

When done with intention and authenticity, mirroring can transform how you connect with others. The next chapter will discuss the final step in building connections: names. Names, which most of us do not control, can be the key to influencing strangers.

LAW 5:

THE NAME CONNECTION

One of the most inevitable aspects of life is interactions. With the increased use of social media and other communication networks, communication has become more profound. We often interact with different people and sometimes find recalling names difficult. But what if I told you there is a way to use *names* as a tool to build lasting connections?

Names are significant parts of our being. They are symbols of our individuality and a big part of our identity. Names are like identification tags that make everyone stand out from the other people around them.

One of the most effective ways to gain someone's attention is by calling out their name. Our brains are wired to respond to the sound of our names by releasing feel-good chemicals like dopamine and endorphins. This cerebral response makes us feel highly engaged and focused on the source.

The name connection illustrates how easily we form bonds when interacting with people while actively trying to remember and address them by their names. This serves as the foundation for creating more potent and longer-lasting relationships. This act makes them pay attention, and generating interest in the people we relate to is necessary.

Why Remembering and Using Someone's Name Matters

Meeting an acquaintance and realizing we can't recall their name while interacting can be quite uncomfortable for both individuals—but even more so for the person whose name you can't recall. It can trigger feelings of being unimportant and make them feel undervalued and unnoticed. This highlights the value of remembering and using someone's name!

Here are some benefits of remembering and using someone's name:

1. **Ease of Breaking into a Conversation:**

   We sometimes find ourselves in situations where we are required to make small talk, and it may be challenging to start the conversation. This is where our important tool comes into play. As previously discussed, our brain registers when someone calls our name, signaling that when someone addresses us by our name, they deserve our attention and are equally attentive to us.

2. **Indicates Respect and Appreciation:**

   When we use someone's name, it sends a powerful signal. Imagine someone you have only met once remembers your name and uses it in conversation. You would feel an instant connection with that person. The first thought might be, *"Oh, they remembered,"* because it shows they cared enough to remember or respected you enough to do so. With strangers, using their names, especially if you have only just learned them, adds a layer of familiarity and respect. As discussed in the chapter on familiarity, communication becomes easier when someone feels warmth or acknowledgment from you.

3. **Builds Relationships and Trust:**

When walking in a crowd, our primary focus is our destination. Many activities might happen, but they don't distract us from where we're going. However, when we hear the sound of our name, we almost automatically search for the source. This is because mentioning our name creates a sense of familiarity, prompting us to want to know who called us. The fact that someone knows our name often makes us more receptive to them. That little knowledge can determine whether we continue walking or stop to engage.

4. **Makes communication easier:**

Addressing people by their names facilitates smoother communication, avoids misunderstandings, and helps convey messages effectively. For instance, in a room full of people, the easiest way to get someone's attention is by saying their name. Conversely, failing to recall or use people's names can make interactions more awkward and less effective.

In his book Never Eat Alone, Keith Ferrazzi said, "If you make a conscious decision to recall names, it shows that you care about them, and the conversation will immediately improve because of it."

Here are some practical tips to help in remembering and using people's names:

1. **Take notice:**

Even with our best efforts, remembering names can be challenging. However, one key factor in successful name retention is intentionality—consciously focusing on and recalling names. When meeting someone new, make a deliberate decision to remember their name. Being intentional about remembering names demonstrates how much you value others, which in turn makes you valuable to them.

2. **Repeat and Rehearse:**

Sometimes, unfamiliar names can be hard to recall, but repeating them in your mind and practicing them in conversation helps strengthen your memory. Research shows that people are happier when they are asked to repeat their names rather than having their names mispronounced or forgotten. The effort it takes to learn a name speaks volumes about the importance given to a person.

3. **Relates it to a Memory:**

Everyone has a unique quality that differentiates them

from others. While you might not always remember a person's name at first, associating a memory or characteristic with them can serve as a reminder and make it easier to recall their name.

4. **Use it now and again:**

As previously mentioned, calling someone by their name grabs their attention. In daily interactions, make it a habit to use a person's name in conversations. This keeps their attention and facilitates smoother communication. Nobody wants to converse with someone whose attention seems divided, but the regular use of a name helps maintain focus and keeps the conversation engaging.

Remembering and using someone's name matters. It seems like a simple act, but it can make a difference in relationships and interactions.

Techniques to Make Others Feel Valued

1. **Listen:**

Home is that place we can't compare to anywhere else; it's our special place where we feel safe and can express ourselves freely. Listening has a similar effect on people. When we become good listeners, we create a space where others feel safe and can freely express themselves. This fosters a sense of value and helps build meaningful connections. On the other hand, ignoring people has the opposite effect, pushing them away. When people feel heard, they are more likely to reciprocate by listening to others, creating a positive cycle of communication and understanding.

2. **Expression appreciation:**

The power of a simple "thank you" cannot be underestimated. Expressing appreciation, no matter how small the gesture, can brighten someone's day and make them feel valued. It doesn't have to be extravagant to leave a significant impact. Showing gratitude not only uplifts others but also fosters mutual respect and a positive rapport, improving relationships for everyone involved.

Before moving to the next part of this book, reflect on everything we've discussed so far. Recall moments when you've successfully built genuine connections with others using these principles. More importantly, consider how you can apply these techniques to make new connections moving forward.

In the next section, we will explore the concept of output trust and its significance in influencing people effectively.

PART II:

GAINING TRUST

LAW 6:

THE POWER OF VULNERABILITY

What is the crucial aspect of any interaction? Trust. Why? It is a catalyst for influence to work. Without trust, you can't successfully persuade a buyer in the market or make a new social connection. You must build trust before starting any relationship because trust is the foundation. People are naturally more likely to be influenced by someone they trust because trust breeds comfort and openness. However, gaining trust doesn't happen automatically, especially when dealing with strangers. It begins with vulnerability.

Vulnerability is the gateway through which you form genuine connections. Your human nature shines through, making you more relatable and trustworthy. In this chapter, we will gain a deep insight into the power of vulnerability, studying how it can help you establish trust quickly and effectively so that it can work.

When you first meet a stranger, there is often an invisible barrier between you and them—a lack of familiarity that makes it difficult to form a connection. To break through this barrier, you need something more than facts or superficial conversation: vulnerability. The sixth law teaches us that allowing yourself to be open and authentic in your interactions with strangers is one way to gain influence.

Allowing yourself to be vulnerable does not mean oversharing your deepest secrets or exposing all your flaws. Instead, you should be honest. Honesty and vulnerability work hand in hand. An honest person is willing to share personal details, which reveals their human side and enables others to connect with them. However, vulnerability is complex. Two key skills are essential: knowing how to share according to the context of the situation and understanding when to share personal stories. Mastering these skills can make it easier to build trust and establish lasting relationships with others, even with strangers.

Sharing appropriately to establish trust

Any meaningful relationship requires trust for it to work, and for trust to work, you must allow yourself to be vulnerable so others may know more about you. However, vulnerability can be uncomfortable when misused. To connect with the other party, you must know how to share parts of yourself appropriately.

People often associate vulnerability with weakness or insecurity, but it is quite the opposite. Being vulnerable shows your strength and willingness to be open and authentic about yourself. It's a good quality, and its bad reputation is something we should discard. By trusting others with details and facts about our personal lives, we invite them to trust us in return. They become more willing to share parts of themselves too.

This reciprocal exchange of trust lays the groundwork for influence to work in a relationship. However, knowing when and how to share is a challenge.

Not all forms of vulnerability are equally effective, so you must learn how to share appropriately. The first step in doing so is understanding your relationship with the other party. Is the person you're speaking to part of a business or casual social interaction? The level of vulnerability you show should correspond to the context of your relationship with the person.

At work, sharing a story about something that happened in your personal and private life may be inappropriate. But if you share a challenge you overcame either at school or at a previous job with someone struggling with, say, their productivity in the office, that type of vulnerability would work because it addresses the issue and fits the context of professional life. You're trying to build a bridge, not a barrier. However, if you cross the line from sharing to oversharing, you will effectively raise a barrier. If you share insecurities about your marriage, for instance, at work, you can create awkwardness. The other person might feel uncomfortable and not know how to respond. This can sour the relationship you are trying to build. The wrong type of vulnerability can cause discomfort instead of safety and trust.

Therefore, you must know your audience and be mindful of boundaries when sharing. By being vulnerable, we create connections with others, not burden them with unnecessary details. Always aim for balance—share just enough to be genuine but don't overwhelm the other person with too much. You build trust slowly, and sharing small pieces of yourself over time can often be more effective than laying it all on the table at once. This process gradually builds mutual respect and understanding, allowing you to guide the other person more effectively.

How to use personal stories to connect

A personal story is one of the best ways to build trust with strangers. We feel connected to stories because they help us relate to others and understand the world. When you share a personal story, you invite your listeners into your world, allowing them to see things from your perspective. Doing so builds rapport, creates empathy, and makes connecting on a deeper level easier. But the key is telling the right story at the right time.

You can use a story about yourself to establish common ground or find shared interests with someone you just met. However, there are two things to consider first: the story you tell and its relevance to the person you are speaking with.

You should ensure the person is likely to relate to the experience you're sharing, or determine if that person works in a similar field where your personal stories might be more relatable. Remember that context is key. A good personal story will enable the listener to see themselves in your shoes, even if they haven't had the same experience.

Personal stories also allow you to showcase your values and character. For example, when talking to a stranger about teamwork, you might recount an experience of working with a group to accomplish a team goal. The listener can see your collaboration and how you overcame challenges. This will help make it easier for them, as they now have a picture of who you are and what you stand for.

However, you must note that your stories need to be engaging to have the maximum effect on your listeners. Do not make them just about you. Storytelling inherently opens space for empathy and understanding, and empathy is key to influence. The point is for the listener to see themselves in your story and create a better connection. So, if a stranger feels they can relate to your experiences or see your values reflected in their own, they are more likely to trust you.

Of course, your personal story should be relevant to the moment. Delivering your story at the right time can transform a bland conversation into something memorable. But if told at the wrong time, it can come off as forced or disjointed, and you don't want that. Timing is a crucial aspect here, as with any form of vulnerability.

Some of the best TED Talks involve a personal story or anecdote. Later in this book, we will adequately discuss the power of storytelling. However, personal stories can break down the subconscious barriers we put up when we talk to strangers. They can create warmth in an otherwise cold interaction.

Once again, I will point out that there is a difference between sharing and hogging a conversation. If you spend the entire time yapping about yourself and not listening to the other person, you just come across as self-centered. Pay attention to their body language and tone. When they stop being interested, drop it. Respect their boundaries and don't make them feel overwhelmed.

So, remember to share appropriately and only in contexts your listener can relate to. As a result, you will have a more meaningful interaction with them and be able to build genuine relationships. Vulnerability is the cornerstone of influence since it builds trust over time. Vulnerability isn't the only way we can build trust. In the next chapter, we will explore the psychological phenomenon known as consistency bias.

LAW 7:

CONSISTENCY BIAS

When someone acts in a way we can predict, we are more likely to trust them. This is the consistency bias. Consistency and predictability create a soft cocoon of comfort that makes us feel safe. When we feel secure, we become more trusting. This bias pays off in almost all human interactions. It plays a crucial role in building trust. Despite our best efforts, we are naturally inclined to trust those whose actions and words match over time, regardless of whether we realize it. This chapter explores how consistency influences our perceptions of others and how you can use this to establish trust.

Human beings are habitual creatures. As such, we tend to feel more comfortable with people who behave in predictable ways. Why? Because it provides a sense of stability and reliability. You do not have to worry if someone will keep their promises if that person consistently does so. You are reassured and feel safe in your interactions and decisions with that person.

This chapter will explore why people prefer to be around predictable individuals and examine how you can leverage consistency bias to build trust with strangers.

Why do people like those who are predictable

Our brains constantly work to make sense of the world around us. We look for patterns and behaviors to help us navigate social interactions. When someone is predictable, we feel confident about what to expect. This comforts us and allows us to build trust because we no longer have to doubt a person's intentions or worry about their promises and inconsistencies.

Take the example of a professional relationship. Predictability is one of the most critical factors in developing trust when meeting a new colleague or business partner. People appreciate knowing that when you make a promise, you will keep it. If you consistently show up on time, follow through on commitments, and act reliably, others will trust you and feel comfortable with your presence.

Psychologically, people prefer predictability because it reduces anxiety. When we interact with someone unpredictable—whether their words don't align with their actions or they often change their stance—we feel uncertain. That uncertainty makes us hesitant to rely on them, and we are left unsure how they will react in particular situations.

This is why we are drawn to consistent individuals. Meeting someone who calmly follows through on their commitments brings peace of mind. You don't have to guess or second-guess with them. You know that what they say is what they mean, and what they mean is what they do. This fosters a sense of safety and security in the relationship.

Suppose you always meet deadlines and respond to emails at work. Over time, your boss will come to expect this behavior. The more they can rely on you, the more they will trust you.

Therefore, your actions must be predictable and consistent in business or social contexts. Consistency in your words and actions will help you appear trustworthy and reliable to others, giving you a better chance of influencing them positively over time.

Building trust through reliability and fol-low-through

People crave predictability, so leveraging this insight to build trust starts with reliability and follow-through. Earning trust takes time and consistency; it requires constant action and repeated evidence of reliability. Whenever you say you will do something and follow through on that commitment, you reinforce the trust others place in you. This reliability creates a solid foundation on which to build influence.

Let's say you're meeting a potential client or business partner for the first time, and you promise to follow up with additional information or set up a future meeting. How you handle this promise is crucial. If you fail to follow through, the trust you've begun to establish with that person can quickly erode. On the other hand, if you consistently deliver on your promises, people will start to trust you more.

People are far more likely to listen to and follow someone they perceive as dependable. If you tell a stranger that you will send them information by a specific time and you consistently do so, they will start to view you as someone they can rely on. Your word becomes a guarantee of action, and this consistency strengthens your influence. Over time, others will associate your name with reliability, and your reputation will grow.

But reliability doesn't stop at keeping promises. It also involves availability. When a child is in trouble, they seek out their mom or dad. Apart from their emotional connection to their parents, they rely on them because they are always around. They know their parents can help them escape trouble because they have always been there. Similarly, if people know they can reach out to you and get a thoughtful response, they will continue to think of you as reliable. You must always be available and present.

Reliability can be an essential tool in gaining trust. People feel secure knowing they can trust and rely on you for timely and consistent action.

When you build trust through reliability, you must always follow through. In other words, make sure you consistently deliver on your promises. Keeping your commitments shows you are serious and reinforces the idea that you can be relied upon. People will begin to trust you because your past actions demonstrate that they can depend on you in the future. As your reputation grows, consistency bias begins to work to your advantage, solidifying your position as "Captain Trustworthy."

In essence, predictability increases others' respect for you. If people trust your judgment and follow your lead, they will likely turn to you for advice. Maintain consistency so people can rely on you and interact comfortably with you. While consistency appeals to the logical and safe parts of the human brain, emotions are arguably even more powerful. In the next chapter, we will discuss emotional contagion and how it can shape our day-to-day experiences.

LAW 8:

EMOTIONAL CONTAGION

Emotions are potent in the social construct and can be a great way to connect with a stranger. People are naturally attuned to the moods and feelings of those around them, even unconsciously mirroring them at times. This phenomenon is known as emotional contagion, which is, to put it better, the ability of emotions to spread from one person to another.

Understanding how emotions affect behavior, reactions, and decisions is essential. Our emotional state can profoundly impact those we interact with, whether we like it or not. You can use it to help or hinder your ability to gain trust.

Your emotional energy can affect your first interactions with strangers. Are you optimistic, calm, and approachable? Or are you anxious, distant, or frustrated? These emotions, whether overt or subtle, are contagious. People tend to pick up on the emotional state of others, and this can shape their perception of you and the trust they are willing to place in you.

This chapter explores how moods and emotions affect others and how emotional contagion can project positive energy, inspire trust, and build a strong connection with a stranger.

How moods and emotions influence others

As social beings, emotions shape how we perceive and react to others. Despite not being conscious of it, people can detect other people's feelings quickly. This means that if you walk into a room with a smile and a positive attitude, there is a high chance that others will also pick up on that behavior. Conversely, if you're tense, anxious, or negative, others may feel uncomfortable, irritated, or uneasy.

This is the power of emotional contagion. It works in two ways: first, we subconsciously pick up on the emotional cues of others; second, our emotional state can trigger similar emotions in the people around us. This makes it essential to be aware of the feelings you're projecting when meeting someone for the first time.

Approaching a stranger with enthusiasm, confidence, and optimism will lead to a positive response. This will make the other person more open and willing to trust you. Your positive emotional energy will create a comfortable atmosphere for agreements and collaborations. So, if you're trying to broker a deal with a potential partner, follow this approach.

On the other hand, if you are anxious or frustrated when meeting a stranger, your body language, tone of voice, and overall demeanor will likely convey your feelings. Negative emotions like that will make the other person uncomfortable or distant.

Emotional contagion isn't limited to face-to-face interactions. It can also take place via virtual communication. Your words and tone can still convey an emotional state, even on a video call or in a text.

For example, if you send an email with an upbeat or encouraging tone, the recipient is more likely to respond positively and openly. But if your message gives off a curt or hostile vibe, it can make the receiver uncomfortable and may lead to distrust. This can all happen in the absence of face-to-face interaction.

Understanding moods and emotions can help you create an atmosphere of trust. By consciously being aware of your emotional state, you can successfully shape the conversation flow, close that business deal, or make a new social connection. Knowing how emotional contagion works can also help you create a meaningful relationship.

Projecting positive energy to inspire trust

Having learned how emotions affect others, the next step is to learn how to project positive energy to gain strangers' trust. The key to positive energy is confidence, calmness, and openness that invites others to feel comfortable around you. Positive energy creates a trust-building environment.

The best way to display positive energy is through optimism; it can be a very contagious attribute. Your "can-do" attitude at work may encourage coworkers to share the same outlook.

Now, you don't need to go to work wearing a fake smile or overly enthusiastic attitude; instead, bring a balanced, positive outlook. When conversations seem negative or uncertain, you can steer them more positively. This can be as simple as maintaining a calm and confident demeanor, highlighting solutions, or emphasizing opportunities.

People trust optimistic individuals, especially if they can maintain optimism in challenging situations. Being calm and collected in chaotic moments creates the belief that you can handle the situation even though it might be more significant than you. Positivity is infectious. If you approach problems with that positive vibe, people begin to trust you to handle more challenges because they feel safe and secure with you.

Another key to projecting positive energy is communication. This can significantly affect how others perceive your emotional state. To project positive energy, you must practice actions like open body language (avoid crossing your arms or looking closed off). Also, remember to smile often and keep your tone warm and approachable. Small gestures during a conversation, such as maintaining eye contact and nodding, can also build trust.

But that's not all. Show interest in what people around you are doing. If you want to make friends with someone, say at a museum, and you see them looking at a particular artifact, asking questions about it is a good way to start the conversation. They will open up to you when you listen and ask them thoughtful questions. This is also known as emotional validation, which encourages them to feel valued and respected. People are likely to trust those who make them feel seen and heard.

Projecting positive energy is about creating a space where the other person feels comfortable and confident in you. When they sense that you are emotionally steady and genuinely interested in their thoughts and feelings, they are far more likely to open up, trust you, and be receptive to you.

Emotional contagion can be a subtle yet impactful force in human interactions. You can create trust and direct a conversation through positive energy. In the same way, you can create discomfort and distance by spreading negative emotions. This will, of course, make it harder for you to be trusted. You should learn to be mindful of your emotional state and how it impacts those around you. This gives you a strategic advantage in influencing a stranger.

LAW 9:

THE PRIMACY EFFECT

The Primacy Effect, also known as primacy bias, is a form of cognitive bias that includes both the Primacy and Recency effects.

The Primacy Effect is a psychological tendency to remember and place more importance on an initial impression or information received about a person. The Recency Effect best describes the psychological tendency to remember the last details of an item or a person. Still, despite its limitations and weaknesses, the Primacy Effect is essential for the success of public relations and social interactions.

German psychologist Hermann Ebbinghaus conducted this revolutionary psychological study and coined the term "the serial position effect."

The Primacy Effect helps in decision-making and the selection of otherwise overwhelming amounts of data we process, primarily due to the limitations of our memory capacity, which can only hold a finite amount of information at any given time. The human brain, although remarkable, has some performance limitations.

William Crano further explained this in his study of the Primacy Effect, in which he mentioned that people often focused more on the beginning of a presentation than the remaining parts of it. However, this significant phenomenon affects how we process information and draw conclusions about others, which can sometimes be biased.

Individuals often favor information that confirms their beliefs and expectations, usually based on an initial impression. Our interpretation of subsequent information heavily relies on an initial judgment in a way that is difficult to alter with new information. In 1980, Dewey Rundus also discussed how the Primacy Effect influences humans through repetition. He believed that humans attempting to memorize or rehearse a list from the beginning repeatedly solidify the first items in their memory.

Despite its disadvantages, the Primacy Effect allows for strategically creating a positive impression in social interactions if used well. As mentioned earlier, knowing how to influence your audience's memory positively requires a careful and strategic presentation, which can help you overcome any biases that might affect how you are perceived.

This chapter will discuss two major strategies for using the Primacy Effect to gain an advantage in social interactions.

The Importance of Starting Strong

There is a famous saying: "You only get one chance to make a first impression." Even though this is not entirely true, it is not entirely wrong. It is important to play our cards right during any interaction, whether in a formal or informal setting, because, in social relationships, first impressions can set the tone for future interactions.

For instance, if people perceive you as warm and friendly during the first encounter, they are more likely to approach you positively in the future. But if you are perceived as the opposite—cold and uptight—you automatically lose more networking opportunities and a good reputation.

Now, to achieve a solid start or impression on someone, there are a few things to consider such as:

- **Being observant** means sizing up an individual, taking in their expression, energy, and response to you. Your choice of words for the first few seconds must portray a sound level of intelligence and observation.

- **Alignment:** With their interests, you're sure you'll be adding to address their needs and not talking to them or speaking to their heads. Also, we tend to be more drawn to people who are similar to ourselves. Now, this doesn't encourage putting on a false display. It is simply to ensure alignment in shared interests with the audience. In a formal setting, for instance, sharing similar goals and interests increases the chances of compatibility and true friendship. Tailoring your speech to specific needs and interests is vital to making a strong first impression. Understanding their preferences, perspectives, and aspirations makes it even easier to create a connection that resonates with them on a deeper level.

- **Authenticity** suggests your emotions should be original, as people are smart enough to see through a facade. By expressing your feelings honestly and openly, using clear communication, expressions, and actions, you gain trust and confidence from a person or people. The strategies mentioned boil down to one sentence: Put your most important messages at the beginning.

You can convey your message verbally and nonverbally; the receiving party might interpret it differently. Make your communication clear and straightforward enough to avoid misinterpretations. Why do I have to go through all the hassle to impress someone?

We have something to gain from them when trying to impress someone. This could be material, such as money, a job promotion, or emotional. We might think they'd make a great friend or partner. Well, this is what happens when you have finally worked your way into leaving your footprints in a person's memory:

- **Confidence:** In an informal setting, applying the above strategies causes the receiving party to subconsciously lower their guard and sets grounds for more openness and honesty. On the other hand, as an individual who has built a strong first impression, you will also experience a boost in confidence. This results in satisfaction and fulfillment, as you know the strong foundation you've set for future interactions.

- **Career Boost:** I mentioned earlier that our desire to impress someone might be for something material, such as a job promotion. Research suggests that about 72% of people we interact with are involved in our careers, especially in career boosts. If you work in a corporate setting, getting a promotion or recognition for your efforts takes more than competence. What people think of you factors into your career trajectory.

Every level we desire to achieve depends on the impressions we leave in people's memories. This is why transparency in your words and actions is essential to gain the trust and reliability of your receiving party.

How To Set The Tone in First Encounters

In this sense, tone is about your voice and how you communicate in general. As you know, communication is both verbal and non-verbal. How you communicate the first encounter matters way more than it should, and we can swim against the tide or use it to our advantage. This section teaches the key parts of communicating if you want to leave a memorable encounter.

- **Physical Appearance:** Your physical appearance is the first thing people notice about you; consequently, it becomes the first thing you communicate. We dress more attractively and pleasantly when we go on a night out or to the club. This is because, in that social setting, we want to communicate attractiveness. When it is cold out, we dress warmly because that is what is required. This applies in professional settings as well. When we have a big presentation or start the first day of a new job, we dress very well and formally because we want people to take us seriously.

- **Gestural communication:** we perform gestures such as body language and facial expressions. According to research by a psychologist known as Albert Mehrabian, gestures communicate more than 50% of a person's actual words and thoughts, while spoken words communicate less than 40%. That is to say that your gestures and emotions communicate bigger chunks of information than you intend to while significantly impacting the impression you make. Standing upright with broad shoulders makes you look strong and reliable when you want people to see you as an authority figure. When people try to hide, they fold in their shoulders, drop the volume of their voice, and even lower their heads. When we see someone pointing towards us and laughing, we interpret it as mockery. Even though we have no idea what they're saying, this is how powerful Nonverbal communication is. Ask yourself what kind of first impression you're looking to make.

- **Verbal Communication.** It is essential to understand that communication is more than just words. Instead, they are more of an opportunity to connect with people on a deeper level. By carefully choosing your opening statement and ensuring engagement from your partner, you build a successful emotional connection, and your words tend to become more impactful and memorable. It is a known fact that the tone doesn't come naturally to most people, which is why there has been much research on it. It involves much practice and is a skill that you learn and hone.

A good way to start is by being self-aware of your personality and emotionally intelligent about people's responses to you. For example, a naturally distant or aloof person can consciously work on smiling more, making eye contact, and engaging in active listening to create a warmer and more approachable impression. This helps us adapt to different characteristics and flow naturally with them.

In conclusion, while first impressions play a significant role in how people form judgments, they do not capture the entirety of a person. However, they set the stage for future interactions.

In the next chapter, we will explore the law of contract and its implications for influencing strangers in a world of choices.

LAW 10:

THE RULE OF CONTRAST

We live in an age with an abundance of choices. From breakfast options to career choices, there is an endless availability of choices. However, our encounters at different stages of life often leave us with specific perspectives that stick around for as long as they can. This is where the Rule of Contrast comes in. It utilizes the weaknesses of our human perspectives, shaping our perceptions and influencing our decisions often without our realization. Because we have such an abundance of choices, we have the same number of decisions to make, and in the fast-paced world we live in, these decisions usually have to be made quickly.

According to psychologists, no decision is purely rational. Emotions, uncertainty, and social influence are essential factors that affect our decision-making process. Understanding the psychology of decision-making ultimately empowers you to make your words count significantly in people's minds.

When applied tactfully and correctly, this rule can answer the silent question we often ask ourselves: Why should people listen to me? This question means more than what it implies. It is not always about being heard or listened to but about why people should trust and apply what you say. In summary, it is, or should be, more of a 'How can I be trusted?' question. Now, this brings us to what the Rule of Contrast is.

The Rule of Contrast is a cognitive bias that affects how we evaluate and compare different options or alternatives. Robert Cialdini, who first studied this rule, explained how it often leads us to assess the lesser or greater value of two things through direct comparison.

Does the contrast principle work? The rule effectively creates a reference point or anchor bound to influence a person's judgment and perception.

When encountering something strange, we naturally want to compare it to something familiar. On a more abstract scale, this leads to seeking out information from the new and unfamiliar to confirm beliefs or ideas that we already hold. We discuss confirmation bias in more detail in our chapter on this topic. By making this comparison, the new thing seems more or less attractive or reasonable depending on how it contrasts with the anchor provided.

The power of contrast lies in its ability to make several appearances with the same information based on our existing perception. This perfectly explains how a person is affected when introduced to two different alternatives, which tend to either distort or amplify our perception of things. By recognizing this principle's solid effect, it becomes easier to connect with people on a much deeper level and exert your influence on them.

One significant result of applying contrast as a psychological tool is its ability to be invisible. The effect of the contrast rule isn't usually known to the object, just to you. The next question you might ask is: 'How do I use the contrast rule as a tool of influence?'

It is also one significant way to quickly gain people's trust, primarily unfamiliar ones, to be heard and have a smooth experience with them anywhere.

Creating a Favourable Impression by Comparison

Applying the contrast principle begins with communicating a favorable impression of yourself. How, then, do we create favorable impressions by comparison?

- **Showcasing your positive traits:**

It involves subtly showing your best characteristics while contrasting them with your less favorable ones. Creating your best impression does not involve wearing a facade but winning a person's trust and confidence by displaying your best characteristics and concealing your less favorable ones. Creating a favorable impression by shielding or holding onto unfavorable information is instinctive. Putting your best foot forward puts you in a better position.

- **Addressing a problem:**

This is often done by painting a vivid picture in your subject's mind and appealing to their emotions. For instance, let's take a moment to observe the tactics of great advertisements and sales write-ups. First, they present a general problem, which makes it about the listener tactfully engaged. Afterward, the consequences of such a problem are shared and emphasized. This isn't because you have been ignorant of the issue, but because sharing the problem creates expectancy for a solution. So what happens next? Now, you want a solution!

If you observe closely, not only was the negative mentioned first, but its impacts also amplified in your audience's mind. This method is based on the fact that what people show us first tends to be more important than what they show us afterward: the primacy effect. For example, if someone shows us a picture of an 'ugly' person first and then a beautiful person next, the ugly person will seem uglier while the beautiful person will seem more attractive. Addressing a problem first naturally enhances it in the minds of your audience. Then, offering a solution becomes much easier for you and the subject involved.

Another crucial point to note is to avoid direct criticism. This means that when pointing out a problem or issue, we should try hard not to belittle the subject. A thin, almost invisible line separates these two worlds, so maintaining balance is essential. Good managers or employers, for instance, are familiar with the compliment sandwich. That is, criticism is served between praise. Instead of saying this thing is terrible, it is more effective to say, "I liked how you started this; how about we try this other instead?" The goal is to appeal to their emotions instead of wounding them.

- **Be Authentic**:

This is the most crucial point. For each comparison you highlight, you should also genuinely appreciate its qualities. Insincere comparisons can come across as manipulation.

Subtle Ways to Appear Approachable and Credible

"Appearance" applies to more than just physical appearance, especially in creating an approachable and credible impression. However, as discussed in the previous chapter, this does not lessen the importance of physical appearance. Now, we will discuss other subtle ways to appear approachable and credible. First, it is crucial to understand the effect of gaining credibility from people.

Gaining credibility is similar to getting their ultimate stamp of approval, which facilitates the flow of influence. Extending control on a person begins with solid credibility grounds, although this usually happens after passing the *'Approachable'* test.

But being approachable and credible work simultaneously. Here is how:

- **Be Easily Accessible.** Building a solid hold over a person starts with being available. This is another way to appeal to a person's emotions. Consistency in physical and otherwise appearance tends to earn you a more trustworthy title easily.

- **Maintain open arms—Before a physi**cal approach from you or to you, maintaining an open posture or stance is often advisable, facilitating fluent communication. One great way to begin is by sharing relatable experiences and providing trusted and approved solutions that apply personally.

In summary, people's assessments and judgments are based on what they see rather than beyond the layers. Gaining and applying this practical knowledge helps you control what you want them to see and why they should trust it.

PART III:

SPARKING INFLUENCE

LAW 11:

THE SOCIAL PROOF RULE

Imagine it is your first time at the airport, and you are confused about where to go. You see fellow travelers like you lugging their bags, eyes fixed on the signs around them. You wonder how they can find their way with so much ease. Suddenly, you spot someone holding a similar ticket and start following them, hoping they will lead you to the right destination. This stranger has just influenced your decision to act. The social proof psychology principle states that when people are uncertain, they will most likely look to others for behavioral guidance.

According to a study by Robert Cialdini, a renowned psychologist and author, 75% of people admit that social proof affects their decision-making ability. Social influence often consciously and subconsciously determines our choices in a world driven by others' opinions. Individuals look to others for guidance on how to behave or make decisions, believing that if others are doing something, it must be the right thing.

It is a potent psychological skill that can significantly influence behavior, especially in uncertain environments. Because humans are social creatures, we look to each other for patterns and cues for direction. Our need to live in groups, cooperate, and follow social norms shapes our evolutionary development and survival as a species. This ingrained social nature plays a pivotal role in how we make decisions, perceive the world, and interact with others, including in the context of consumer behavior.

Humans evolved in social environments where cooperation was key to survival. Early human ancestors lived in groups for mutual protection, hunting, and gathering. Social cohesion and the ability to function well within a group were critical to securing resources and avoiding danger. As a result, humans developed a strong tendency to rely on social cues and shared practices to guide behavior and decision-making. We can trace how we interact socially to our evolutionary history, where individuals living together as groups provided advantages such as protection, resource sharing, and the ability to tackle challenges collaboratively. In prehistoric times, if one person found a safe place to locate food or water, others would likely follow, trusting the first person's judgment because it helped ensure safety and survival. The same principle applies to how people today make decisions—we often look to others for cues on what is safe, desirable, or beneficial. Cooperation within a group meant people needed to trust each other's actions.

Social connections influence almost every aspect of our lives, from behavior and emotions to decision-making and identity formation. We form groups, societies, and networks for mutual support, cooperation, and shared goals.

Key Components of Social Proof Theory

1. Conformity and Bandwagon Effect:

Conformity is the tendency of individuals to adjust their behavior to match that of a group they identify with, often due to a desire to be accepted. Humans have an innate desire to belong to a community, and as a result, we usually conform to the behavior of others. If we see many people engaging in a particular behavior, we may feel compelled to follow suit, believing their actions reflect the correct course. It is why we unconsciously join long queues when we do not know where to go or order the same meal and are confused about what to eat or when fashion trends are popular. This behavior stems from the human need for social acceptance. When in doubt, people often look to others for guidance, believing that following the majority's actions is the safest or most appropriate choice. You are planning a special dinner with friends and want to select a restaurant that guarantees a delightful experience.

2. **Informational Social Influence:**

Social influence occurs when individuals rely on others' actions or opinions to make decisions in uncertain or ambiguous situations. When we do not have enough information to make an informed decision, we look at what others are doing. For example, if you are in a new city and see a long line outside a restaurant, you might assume that the restaurant is good, even if you are unfamiliar with its food or quality. The line serves as social proof that others have found it worth waiting. People assume that others have more knowledge, so they use others' behavior to guide their decisions. We read reviews online before we buy a product or patronize a new brand. We will read the comments on a viral X post. We look up movie and book reviews; The result now helps us choose.

3. **Normative Social Influence:**

When young and in an unfamiliar social situation, we look to our parents to tell us how to behave. Slowly but surely, the answers that give us become the norm we practice. Now we know what to say at a party or work. We do this because we fear rejection; the outlier is less likely to be liked and accepted.

4. **Crowd behavior:**

The actions of large groups of people can create powerful social proof. Crowd behavior is a form of social proof where large groups of people's actions signal correct behavior. The larger the crowd or the more widespread the behavior, the stronger the social proof. Whether it is a protest, a trend, or simply a group of people choosing a particular brand, the larger the group involved, the more influence it has on others. People tend to believe it must be the correct or socially approved action if many individuals do something. This effect can become even more potent in high visibility or social media amplification situations.

It is a powerful tool for understanding human behavior. It highlights how the behavior of those around us influences our decisions and actions. From conformity to expert advice and crowd behavior, the psychological mechanisms behind these components help explain why humans tend to look to others in ambiguous situations, trust authoritative figures, and often follow the masses. Recognizing these dynamics can help us navigate social situations and make informed decisions.

Creating a Sense of Popularity or Approval

Social proof is a powerful tool to influence strangers, particularly in marketing, sales, or persuasive contexts. Strangers typically have no prior relationship or personal context with the person trying to influence them. Therefore, they may rely more on social cues, such as seeing others engaging with a product or idea, to make decisions. Suppose a stranger considers a product or service widely used or endorsed by others, such as testimonials, user reviews, or social media mentions. In that case, they are more likely to be influenced to try it themselves. This is because humans tend to trust the collective judgment of others over individual opinions in uncertain situations. Strangers often look to the actions of a group for cues on what is socially acceptable or desirable. Suppose they observe a group of people engaging with something, especially in a public setting (e.g., buying from a particular brand or attending an event). In that case, they are more likely to be influenced by that behavior. When an influencer or someone with authority (e.g., an expert) shares positive opinions or experiences about a product or service, strangers are more likely to be persuaded to follow their lead. This is especially effective when we believe that a person is credible, so this type of social proof goes hand in hand with a theory we have already discussed: the consistency bias.

Seeking Acceptance and Conformity through the Agents of Socialisation

Agents of socialization are the individuals, groups, or institutions that influence an individual's social development, values, beliefs, and behaviors. These agents influence how people learn about their culture, societal norms, and societal roles. The main agents of socialization include:

1. **Family:**

   The family is the primary agent of socialization. In the family, individuals first learn language, basic norms, values, and behavior patterns. Family members have a significant impact on social identity and early childhood development. For instance, when people want to get married or choose a college major, they look to their family. When making important decisions, we often turn to our family, maybe parents or siblings, for help.

2. **Peers:**

   Peers are individuals of the same age or social group who influence a person's behavior, interests, and opinions. Peer groups play a critical role in the lives of teenagers. They shape their identities and influence their choice and behaviors, too. They are significant evidence of social proof and powerfully employ social proof. For example, in adolescence, individuals may adopt certain behaviors or attitudes because they see their peers doing the same. Whether it's fashion trends or music preferences, people often conform to what others do, assuming that "everyone else" is doing it for a good reason. This can act as a form of social proof.

3. **Culture and Social Institutions:**

Cultural institutions, such as sports or arts centers, can re-inforce social roles and expectations and shape individual behavior and values.

Social proof operates on the principle that individuals tend to follow the lead of others, assuming that those actions reflect appropriate behavior, particularly when uncertain about what to do. As part of socialization, social proof underscores how individuals look to others to guide their behaviors and conform to group norms, attitudes, and practices perceived as socially acceptable or popular.

LAW 12:

SCARCITY PRINCIPLE

Imagine walking into a store only to see a sign that says, "Only a few left in stock!" Instantly, you feel an urgency to grab the item before it is gone. One of the most influential psychological principles that drives this powerful reaction is scarcity. Our brains are hardwired to perceive scarce commodities as more valuable, and this instinct shapes our buying habits and how we influence others. When we interact with strangers in social settings or professional environments, the perception of scarcity can drastically affect our ability to persuade and connect. From creating a sense of urgency to triggering feelings of exclusivity, scarcity is a tool you can use to influence decisions and behaviors. In this chapter, we will explore how the principle of scarcity operates in human psychology and how you can use it to influence strangers effectively.

In his book, author and psychologist Robert Cialdini said we value opportunities more when they are less available. Have you ever gone to buy a product online only to have a ticking timer pop up, counting down the seconds you have left to finish the order? Your heart rate increases. Adrenaline starts pumping through your veins. You rapidly type out your credit card details and wonder how a little timer could dramatically impact your body; you're feeling the scarcity principle in action. A "one-time-only" event seems more valuable than an event that happens every week. A "limited-edition" sneaker is more desirable than last year's mainstream edition, all because of the scarcity principle.

The psychology of influence is a powerful tool for shaping human behavior. One of the most compelling factors driving our decisions is the scarcity principle, rooted in economics and psychology. The scarcity principle suggests that when humans perceive a commodity as scarce or in limited supply, it becomes more desirable, triggering a sense of urgency and a stronger desire to acquire it. These psychological instincts are not limited to purchasing decisions but extend to our interactions with others, particularly when influencing strangers.

Understanding scarcity can significantly influence how we communicate, persuade, and establish connections with strangers, whether in social situations, marketing, or negotiations. In this chapter, we will explore how the principle of scarcity influences strangers, examining its psychological underpinnings and how we can leverage it to shape behaviors and decision-making.

For example, phrases like "limited-time offer" or "only a few left in stock" trigger feelings of scarcity, leading consumers to secure the item or service before it's gone quickly. Scarcity can apply to physical items (like rare collectibles or limited-edition products) or even non-material things (such as time, attention, or opportunities). It is a key factor in influencing behavior, as people often want what they believe they cannot easily have or what others are competing to have.

Why People Desire What's Limited

Humans experience psychological scarcity when they perceive a lack or limitation in various physical, social, and mental aspects. This scarcity affects their behavior, thoughts, and relationships and is closely tied to fulfilling their psychological needs. Abraham Maslow's Hierarchy of Needs provides a framework for understanding human psychological needs. Maslow organized these needs into a pyramid: at the base are physiological needs (food, water, shelter), followed by safety needs (security, stability), social needs (love, belonging), esteem needs (respect, recognition), and self-actualization needs (personal growth, fulfilling one's potential).

You must be aware of a person's psychological needs to influence them. Humans are motivated to fulfill these needs. When any need goes unmet, people experience a sense of scarcity and inadequacy. For example, when a person's social needs for love and belonging are unfulfilled, they experience emotional deprivation, leading to loneliness, anxiety, or depression. Similarly, when people feel their esteem needs are unmet, they may struggle with feelings of worthlessness or insignificance.

The concept of "man as a creature of scarcity" concerning psychological needs refers to the idea that humans often experience a sense of lack, limitation, or insufficiency in various aspects of their psychological and emotional lives. This scarcity can manifest in different forms, and how it affects our behavior, thoughts, and relationships is deeply intertwined with understanding our psychological needs.

Class of Needs

1. **Physiological Needs**

The most basic needs in Maslow's hierarchy, physiological needs, must be met before we can address higher needs. When people lack essential resources like food, shelter, or sleep, they experience physical and emotional distress. For example, when we are hungry or sleep-deprived, it becomes difficult to focus on anything except settling the need.

2. **Safety Needs (Security, Stability):**

Humans also need safety and security, both physically and emotionally. Scarcity in this area leads to fear and anxiety, often manifesting as an inability to plan or feel at ease. Statistics show that living in a war zone or a high-crime neighborhood reduces a person's chances of maintaining a job or relationship. The emotional strain from the scarcity of safety consumes their psychological resources, leaving them in a constant state of alertness.

3. **Social Needs (Love, Belonging):**

Humans have an inherent need for social connection. When individuals experience a scarcity of love or belonging, they often feel lonely, rejected, or disconnected from others. A person struggling to form meaningful friendships or maintain intimate relationships may experience emotional loneliness, leading to low self-worth. This scarcity of social connection affects their mental health, leading to depression, anxiety, and difficulty engaging with the world around them.

4. **Esteem Needs (Respect, Recognition):**

Esteem needs, which involve feeling valued and respected by others, are critical. Scarcity in this area can lead
to feelings of inferiority, inadequacy, and low self-esteem.
A person constantly feeling unappreciated at work may
experience emotional burnout and lack motivation. If their
achievements go unnoticed, they may appear invisible or
unworthy. Over time, this scarcity of validation can erode
their confidence and hinder their ability to seek new opportunities, contributing to a cycle of negative thinking.

5. **Self-Actualization (Personal Growth, Fulfillment):**

Self-actualization refers to the need to achieve one's fullest
potential. Scarcity in this area can leave individuals feeling unfulfilled or stuck in their personal development. An
artist who lacks the time, resources, or emotional support
to pursue their creative passion may feel frustrated and
unaccomplished. This scarcity of opportunities to express
themselves can lead to dissatisfaction, even if other basic
needs are met. The lack of self-expression hampers their
ability to feel truly fulfilled.

Psychological Scarcity and Motivation

The concept of psychological scarcity also emphasizes how the
perception of limited resources (time, attention, or cognitive re
sources) shapes human behavior. When individuals feel they
are running out of emotional, social, or mental resources, they
may prioritize immediate needs over long-term goals, resulting
in stress, poor decision-making, or maladaptive behaviors. Psy-

chological scarcity influences how people prioritize their goals. When resources such as mental energy, attention, or time are scarce, people become preoccupied with immediate concerns, often neglecting long-term goals. This can affect decision-making and behavior.

- **Cognitive Load:**

When psychological resources like mental energy or focus are scarce, people might struggle to make decisions, solve problems, or think creatively. This creates a sense of mental scarcity, where individuals are preoccupied with their immediate needs, neglecting long-term well-being. Mental scarcity happens when a person feels they lack enough cognitive resources (e.g., attention, memory, focus) to handle the demands placed on them. A college student facing multiple deadlines, exams, and personal issues may feel overwhelmed by cognitive load. The scarcity of mental resources leads to poor decision-making, procrastination, or focusing on the immediate task rather than long-term academic success. Their mental energy is consumed by urgent pressures, making it hard to plan or think creatively.

- **Scarcity Mindset:**

The scarcity mindset arises when people believe they have limited mental, social, or financial resources. This belief causes them to focus excessively on what they lack rather than what they have. The idea of a scarcity mindset suggests that when people perceive their psychological resources as limited (e.g., time, energy, love, or status), they may become anxious or stressed about their ability to meet those needs. This can lead to a focus on short-term gratification, creating cycles of frustration, stress, and dissatisfaction. A person facing financial difficulties might become so focused on immediate survival that they cannot plan for their future or feel hopeful about long-term solutions. They may make impulsive decisions, such as taking on debt to meet current needs, which only exacerbates the scarcity. The constant stress of lacking money dominates their thinking and behavior, making it difficult to focus on improving their situation.

- **Social and Emotional Scarcity**

Humans are social creatures, and emotional and social needs are central to psychological health. Scarcity in these areas can lead to isolation, depression, and anxiety. In human evolution, social connection is vital for survival, and the need for social interaction remains a crucial psychological driver.

- **Scarcity of Social Connection:**

When people lack meaningful relationships or support networks, they feel emotionally isolated. Individuals experience a lack of emotional connection or support; they can feel isolated or rejected. This emotional scarcity can lead to feelings of loneliness and anxiety, affecting mental health and overall well-being. Consider an older person living alone after the loss of a spouse. The scarcity of social connection may lead to loneliness, which can cause feelings of sadness, decreased physical health, and even cognitive decline. The emotional isolation affects their overall well-being and can hinder their ability to pursue other goals, such as personal growth or achieving a sense of accomplishment.

- **Attachment Theory:**

Attachment theory posits that humans have a deep need for secure emotional bonds. When individuals experience a scarcity of attachment, they often develop anxiety or insecurity. Humans are wired to seek and maintain emotional bonds with others. Scarcity in attachment (such as the absence of a supportive relationship) can create feelings of insecurity, anxiety, and longing, influencing mental and emotional stability. A child who grows up in an environment where emotional bonding with caregivers is inconsistent or neglectful may develop attachment issues. As an adult, they may struggle with relationships, often feeling insecure, afraid of abandonment, or unable to trust others. The scarcity of emotional security in early life creates long-lasting effects on their ability to form healthy, stable relationships.

- **Scarcity and the Desire for Achievement:**

Humans naturally seek achievement, success, and recognition, which can lead to feelings of inadequacy and frustration when these are scarce. We often seek self-improvement, success, or recognition. A sense of scarcity can emerge when we don't fulfill these desires.

- **Achievement Scarcity:**

People might feel inadequate or unfulfilled if they cannot achieve personal goals or success. This scarcity of achievement can create stress, dissatisfaction, and frustration, driving individuals to work harder or pursue external validation to overcome the feeling of inadequacy. For example, a sportsperson who constantly practices and fails may feel like a failure.

Scarcity as a Motivator

Despite the distress caused by scarcity, it can also motivate people to act, adapt, and innovate. When individuals experience a lack of resources, they become more resourceful, creative, or determined to fulfill their needs. While psychological scarcity can create distress, it can also motivate. Lacking something can drive individuals to take action, develop resilience, or strive toward self-improvement. In this way, scarcity can act as a catalyst for personal growth, creativity, and problem-solving. However, too much perceived scarcity can overwhelm and lead to adverse outcomes.

Psychological scarcity profoundly shapes our emotions, thoughts, and behaviors. When individuals experience a lack of social connection, mental resources, achievement, or emotional fulfillment, they often become preoccupied with these deficiencies, which can limit their ability to focus on long-term goals or personal growth. However, scarcity can also drive motivation, creativity, and resilience, pushing individuals to find new ways to meet their needs. Understanding how scarcity affects human behavior is key to addressing its impacts and fostering healthier emotional and psychological well-being.

The scarcity principle is a psychological concept that suggests people perceive things as more valuable when they are scarce or in limited supply. To influence strangers using this principle, you can subtly highlight the limited availability of a product, opportunity, or resource, making it seem more desirable. Here are some effective strategies:

1. **Create a Sense of Urgency**

   • **Limited-Time Offers:** Communicate that an offer or opportunity is only available briefly. For example, "This sale ends at midnight," or "Only 10 spots left for this exclusive event."

   • **Countdowns:** Use countdown timers or phrases like

"Hurry, limited-time discount!" This puts pressure on the stranger to act quickly.

2. **Highlight Low Stock or Availability**

• **Limited Quantities:** If you sell something, mention how many items you have left in stock, such as "Only five left in stock" or "Only two tickets remaining." This triggers a fear of missing out (FOMO), a natural emotional response when we believe we're missing out on something valuable. Psychologically, people have a strong drive to avoid regret, so they are more likely to act when they think they might miss an opportunity.

• **Exclusive Access:** This suggests that something is exclusive or rare. For example, on Black Friday, an ad says, "This is a one-time opportunity you would not want to miss."

3. **Leverage Social Proof**

• **What Others Are Doing:** Point out that other people are also interested in or purchasing the item. For example, "X number of people have already signed up today" or "This item is flying off the shelves."

• **Scarcity + Popularity:** When something is scarce and popular, it increases its perceived value. You could say, "This is the last chance to grab one before they're gone—everyone is buying it right now!"

4. **Offer an Exclusive Deal**

- **Invite-Only or Member-Only:** Position an offer as exclusive. For example, "This offer is only available to our special members" or "You're one of the lucky few invited to get early access."

- **Unique Experiences:** Frame an experience or product as something that cannot be found elsewhere, such as "This is a limited edition product available only to a select group."

5. **Utilize FOMO (Fear of Missing Out)**

- **Missed Opportunities:** Make people feel they might miss something great. For example, "Once this event is over, you won't be able to sign up again."

- **Imagery and Phrasing:** Use language that evokes regret, such as "Imagine looking back and realizing you missed this."

6. **Frame in Terms of Exclusivity**

- **Special Access:** Make strangers feel part of a select group. For instance, "Only a few people can access this offer."

- VIP Status Gives the impression that the person is being offered something rare or high status that others cannot obtain.

7. **Make it Appear as an Opportunity for Growth.**

• **Limited Offers That Can Improve Their Life:** Frame an offer as something that could change their life but is only available briefly. For example, "This opportunity could change everything for you, but you must act fast."

• **Time-Sensitive Events or Offers:** Frame events or offers as chances to gain knowledge, experience, or access to something that will enrich their lives, but only for a limited time.

8. **Testimonial & Social Proof**

• **Highlight Others' Success:** Share stories of how others have benefited from the opportunity or product and imply that the chance to achieve similar success is fleeting.

• **Public Endorsement:** Mention any public figures or experts who support the offer or product, making it seem more desirable because of the limited availability.

LAW 13:

ANCHORING EFFECT

If you step into a coffee shop on a chilly morning, you see a sign that reads, "Large coffee: $5.99." It is a price you are accustomed to seeing and feels fair. As you walk down the street to a different café, the barista there offers you a similar large coffee for $7.50. Despite the price difference, you hesitate less than you might have expected. Why? Because that initial $5.99 price has anchored your perception of what is reasonable, even though both coffees are identical. This is the anchoring effect in action. A cognitive bias is where the first piece of information you encounter — in this case, the price — influences your subsequent judgments and decisions.

The anchoring effect extends far beyond simple pricing. It is a powerful psychological skill that can influence decision-making and interactions with people, especially when those people are strangers. We rely on an anchor when negotiating a salary at a new job or haggling at the market. In this example, these anchors can be the initial salary on the listing or the price we heard from someone else. Understanding this bias can empower individuals to make more informed choices and help those looking to influence others, as they can strategically set the anchor to nudge decisions in their favor.

Chapter 9 discussed the primacy effect, arguing that initial information dramatically influences people's judgments. It doesn't matter whether this information is essential; what matters is that it is first. Once the anchor is set, people tend to adjust around it, but they often do not change enough, leading to biased decisions.

Influence of Anchoring on Decision-Making

Have you ever been stuck, wondering what to eat? Sometimes, even those little and seemingly inconsequential decisions can take so long. How much more for a big one? Oftentimes, people experience something called decision fatigue. After all, if you don't make any decisions, you won't have any consequences.

"It is normal to experience many different emotions when deciding. It is common to experience fear, worry, and sometimes even regret. It's rare to find anyone who has gone through life without regretting anything." In a world flooded with data and rapid decision-making, the anchoring effect is one of the most subtle and impactful psychological phenomena guiding human behavior. This cognitive bias causes people to rely heavily on the first piece of information offered—the "anchor"—when making decisions. While often underappreciated, anchoring is a fundamental driver in fields ranging from sales to strategy and can shape consumer behavior and influence corporate success in surprising ways. Because decision-making can be an upheaval task, the anchoring effect can influence strangers in various ways, often unconsciously, in different contexts such as negotiations, sales, and decision-making.

Anchoring can be both a competitive advantage and a hidden risk. Here is a closer look at how it affects various business dimensions:

1. **Sales and Pricing:**

The anchoring effect is crucial in sales. For example, suppose a high price is the first number shown. Customers might assess other options based on this initial reference, perceiving lower-priced alternatives as better value, even if they would not have considered them otherwise. You might not have noticed, but most retail stores display the sales price of an item next to the original price. Instead of just saying this item is on sale, they give you a price you can latch onto. Now that I have mentioned it, you can think of several examples. That way, they set an anchor that you subconsciously rely on.

2. **Negotiations:**

Whether closing a deal with a supplier or pitching to investors, the initial terms or figures often set an anchor that shapes the negotiation trajectory. A perceptive negotiator will anchor high (or low, depending on the context), knowing that this initial anchor will guide the negotiation toward a more favorable outcome of options. Effective leaders leverage this by anchoring discussions around positive goals and high benchmarks, encouraging a team mindset that reaches for more significant consequences. A well-informed negotiator will anchor high (or low, depending on the context), knowing that this initial anchor will guide the negotiation toward a more favorable outcome.

3. **Market Positioning:**

Anchoring also affects how customers perceive your brand. A well-placed message or a bold statement on what you stand for can anchor your brand image. This, in turn, influences customer expectations and purchasing decisions over time, making anchoring a powerful tool in positioning and branding strategies. Sellers can exploit this by setting low starting prices, which attracts more bids. Even though the item may eventually sell for a much higher price, the anchor of the low starting bid drives more engagement.

Using Anchoring to Drive Positive Business Outcomes

Now that we have identified how anchoring can influence decisions, how can leaders use this knowledge strategically and responsibly?

- **Establish High Benchmarks:** In performance management, for instance, set ambitious goals that anchor your team. The initial high benchmark can influence team members to aspire beyond what they may have set for themselves.

Structure Decision-Making Frameworks: Leaders should recognize when anchoring is in play, especially in strategic discussions or financial planning. Leaders can guide teams toward decisions aligned with long-term goals rather than reactive tendencies by setting a balanced and strategic anchor in these conversations.

- **Empower Consumers with Information Anchors**: Businesses that lead with transparency create an informed anchor in consumers' minds. For example, highlighting the sustainability or quality of materials anchors your product's value beyond just price, encouraging customers to assess it with those values in mind.

- **Cultivate Awareness of Anchoring Bias:** Cultivating self-awareness around anchoring can help leaders counter its adverse effects, such as confirmation bias. Train teams to question initial information, seek alternative perspectives, and use data-driven insights to challenge their assumptions.

With great power comes great responsibility, and anchoring is no different. While this cognitive tool can shape decisions, you must apply it ethically. Anchoring should guide individuals toward decisions that benefit them and the organization holistically—not exploit them. Misusing anchoring by setting unrealistic expectations or anchoring around misleading information can erode trust and damage long-term relationships. The key to ethical anchoring is transparency, accountability, and a commitment to one's core values. One can influence outcomes and create an intentional, purpose-driven leadership culture by anchoring decisions to clear shared goals.

LAW 14:

FRAMING EFFECT

While doing your groceries, you see two different milk products. Both cost and weigh the same. One is labeled "80% lean," and the other "20% fat." When comparing the two, you feel that 20% fat sounds unhealthy, so you choose the 80% lean option. There is no difference between the two products, but one sounds more appealing than the other due to the framing effect. The framing effect occurs when people react differently to something depending on whether it is presented as positive or negative.

The framing effect can affect our decision-making skills and our ability to influence the decisions of others. Decision-making is influenced by how the information is presented rather than what a person sees or hears. People are biased toward picking an option they view as a gain over one they view as a loss, even if both options lead to the same result. They are also more likely to make a riskier decision when the option is presented as a gain instead of a loss. The framing effect is a type of cognitive bias or error in thinking. "Framing" refers to whether an option is presented as a negative or a positive. This awareness can make us more thoughtful and less likely to fall for tricks that might lead us to make decisions not in our best interest. Differences in messages stress the positive consequences of performing an act as opposed to the negative impacts of performing a goal or not.

When a statement is framed positively, it may invoke a feeling of safety or gain, whereas when the same statement is framed negatively, it may invoke a sense of loss or danger. This is because emotional reactions and mental shortcuts, or heuristics, are the psychological devices behind the framing effect. This taps into our natural tendency to welcome gains and avoid losses, superseding more logical thinking and leading people to make decisions based on how something feels rather than how it is. Take the above example of 90% fat-free cold cuts versus 10% fat cold cuts. Your choice might not be logical but instead driven by your emotional reaction to the advertiser's choice of words.

Types of Framing

1. Positive Framing:

Have you seen one of those Black Friday ads that tell you, "Order now and save 30 dollars" or something like that? Well, those ads are an example of positive framing. Positive framing highlights the benefits of a given scenario, encouraging us to focus on the optimistic and making us willing to take action. How you present information emphasizes the benefits or outcomes rather than the negative ones. When you frame a statement positively, the focus is on the potential gains, benefits, or positive outcomes rather than the risks, losses, or negative aspects. Positive framing often leads to more significant results. When people see a potential benefit, they are more likely to act to attain it.

Positive framing is vital in making and influencing decisions because individuals tend to be less risk-averse when we frame outcomes positively. People are likely to choose an option that offers a potential benefit, even if it involves some risk. For instance, in medical communication, a doctor framing treatment as a "90% success rate" rather than a "10% failure rate" leads to more favorable decisions. The message about a new treatment framed as "90% success rate" rather than "10% failure rate" leads to a more favorable decision. Positive framing increases optimism bias. This can help boost confidence and action but may also lead to confident decisions without proper consideration of risks and increase collaboration between parties.

2. **Negative framing:**

Negative framing highlights what could go wrong and the losses that may incur if a person does not take the desired action. This kind of framing makes people afraid of the consequences of what will happen if they do not make the desired decision, and it can make people more risk-averse. For example, a parent promising to punish a child if they stay out too late. People react to negative framing differently, developing a sense of protection from harm. A loss is psychologically more painful than an equivalent gain is pleasurable. People are more sensitive to losses than to gains of the same magnitude, making losses psychologically more painful.

When a statement is framed negatively, individuals become more focused on avoiding losses rather than pursuing gains, leading them to make more conservative or risk-averse decisions. People avoid making decisions because they are overwhelmed by the perceived risks and negative consequences. This is particularly true when the framing makes the potential loss seem inescapable or extreme—for example, warning signs to stay off military property. Individuals may feel compelled to act to avoid the perceived moral or social cost, even if doing so is not in their best interest, especially when the price is too high.

3. **Comparative Framing:**

Comparative framing is a comparison of objective information. Comparison framing can influence our choices by comparing facts in a way that makes the preferred perspective more desirable than the alternative. How information is presented compared to other options, situations, or benchmarks can significantly influence how people make decisions. The comparison framing effect highlights differences or similarities between choices, shaping attitudes, judgments, and behaviors in subtle but powerful ways. The negotiator often presents a specific reference point against which other options are compared. This reference point can influence people's perceptions of the value or desirability of the alternatives. The possibilities are usually negative against positive options. Comparative framing can also be based on the anchoring effect. The first option presented in comparative framing often serves as this anchor, affecting subsequent judgments. For illustration, if an expensive car is shown first in a line-up of cars during a car exhibition, people may view other, less costly cars as better deals, even if the price difference is insignificant. Sometimes, comparison framing is presented as a decoy. This is known as the decoy effect.

The Decoy effect occurs when a less attractive option (the decoy) is introduced to make another option seem more desirable. For example, if a customer is presented with two options—one slightly cheaper and one significantly more expensive—and then a third option that is somewhat more expensive than the first but less expensive than the second, the third option would make the middle option look more attractive. In comparative framing, highlighting potential losses compared to a benefit (a negative-framed message) can evoke stronger reactions.

Effects Comparison Framing on Decision-Making:

1. **Choice Overload:** When too many options are presented in a comparative context, people experience "choice overload," which can lead to indecision or suboptimal choices. Having too many options to compare may cause stress or overwhelm decision-making.

2. **Risk Perception:** Framing comparisons in terms of risk can alter how people evaluate uncertainty. For instance, if a specific investment option is framed as having a lower risk than another, people may prefer it even if both have the same risk level but are presented differently.

3. **Decisions Based on Relative Value:** People often make decisions based not on the absolute value of an option but on its relative value compared to others. For instance, people may choose the second-best option in a set of

options because they perceive it as the most "valuable" in comparison rather than evaluating it individually.

4. **Context Effects:** How a statement is presented compared to other options can create a bias in decision-making. A typical example is the "contrast effect," where people perceive something as better or worse depending on its framed context. For example, a restaurant might seem better than one with a very low rating, but it could seem worse than another with a better rating.

5. **Social Comparisons:** Comparative framing can influence social proof decisions, where people make decisions based on how they compare. For instance, salary comparisons can affect decisions related to job offers, and social media comparisons may influence purchasing or lifestyle choices.

Content Presentation

The presentation of options is the most important aspect of framing effect. While content is undeniably essential, the presentation can shape how people perceive, interpret, and act upon that content.

1. **Influence of Perception:** People are more likely to be influenced to make decisions based on how information is presented. For example, if a health treatment is presented as having a "90% success rate," people are more inclined to view it favorably than if it is framed as having a "10% failure rate," even though both frames convey the same underlying statistic—the importance of positive or nega-

tive framing taps into people's emotions and unconscious biases.

2. **Emotional Appeal:** Presentation often evokes emotions, which can drive decision-making more strongly than raw facts. A well-framed statement that evokes fear, hope, or excitement can make the information more impactful and relevant to an individual. For instance, political speeches or posters that use emotional storytelling can override more analytical or objective discussions.

3. **Simplification of Complex Information:** Presentation can make complex information more understandable. By emphasizing specific options or framing them in a way that aligns with people's pre-existing beliefs or desires, the content becomes easier to understand and more appealing. This is why branding, advertising, and even political discourse often focus as much on the how of the message as on the what.

4. **Cognitive Load:** Simple and engaging information reduces the cognitive load for the audience. People process information more easily when framed in a way congruent with their mental models. For example, visual aids, narratives, or metaphors can make the content more relatable, enhancing retention and decision-making.

5. **Context Matters:** The context and environment in which information is presented play a crucial role in its perception. Though the content is identical, the context (e.g., in a formal setting, a friendly conversation, or a media presentation) can significantly alter how it's perceived and received.

Shaping Perceptions through Strategic Messaging.

The entire purpose of the framing effect is to shape perception. Perception is shaped through strategic presentation, and the
framing effect involves how information is presented to influence
public opinion, attitudes, or behaviors. By framing messages in
particular ways, negotiators can shape attitudes, decisions, and
behaviors, often without the audience even recognizing how much
influence the framing has on their thinking. Carefully crafting and
delivering information influences how an audience views a particular issue, person, product, or organization, aligning the audience's thoughts, beliefs, and attitudes with specific outcomes
desired by the communicator. Understanding the target audience's values, principles, preferences, and concerns is essential. A
good communicator recognizes that different groups may require
different messages. Thus, effective strategic messaging is based
on information segmentation. Communications can be designed
to resonate emotionally or appeal to reason, depending on the
audience. Emotional appeals leverage fear, joy, or empathy, while
cognitive appeals may focus on logic, data, or evidence. Therefore,
the purpose of the information should be clear, concise, and consistent.

Awareness of how a person or corporation presents information,
considering alternative perspectives, and asking yourself how
someone else might frame the same information can help you
see through the bias and communicate better. The framing effect
emphasizes how the presentation of information can significantly influence people's decisions and perceptions. Understanding
specific characteristics or wording messages in particular ways
can sway individuals into making choices that may not align with

their initial preferences. This cognitive bias underlines the importance of how a piece of information is framed in decision-making
processes, especially in areas such as marketing, politics, and
media. Understanding the framing effect is crucial for making
informed, unbiased choices in everyday life and can be used to
influence your spouse, your children, your parents, your friends,
or your colleagues. For example, telling children that vegetables
make them more potent than their favorite superheroes can be
an effective strategy. Be aware of how information is presented
in different contexts, perform your research, and think critically
about how information is being framed.

LAW 15:

THE POWER OF CURIOSITY

One of the most powerful tools we have is our curiosity. Curiosity is the strong desire to know or learn something. In every facet of our lives, a mindset of curiosity gives us the opportunity for great success. Curiosity is about having an affinity to seek new experiences, knowledge, and feedback while remaining open to change. It can help us grow, build relationships with others, adapt more effectively to change, and create more innovative solutions. For these reasons, developing a mindset of curiosity can help you and your team be even more successful.

What curiosity means for us

Curiosity triggers the mind, pushing us to explore, question, and discover. It drives us to break barriers, challenge conventions, and seek new perspectives. We move onward, finding hidden truths and unraveling endless possibilities. It ignites our creativity, sharpens our problem-solving skills, and transforms ordinary moments into extraordinary opportunities for growth. Behavioral scientist and management expert Francesca Gino wrote that "maintaining a sense of wonder" is critical to innovation. Being curious is a characteristic of critical thinking and a desire to know more. It is not just about learning information; it is about savoring it. Curious people are compelled to ask questions and comprehend things on both a macro and micro level, allowing them to find solutions where others only see problems.

Curiosity is the ignition of inspiration. It turns a simple idea into a flourishing moment of engagement and imagination. It is the "Why?" and the "How?" we ask when we find inspiration. To learn to be curious, we must leave our comfort zone and try something new—a new hobby, visit a new place, or read about something we do not know. Question everything—even what you think you know. Observe your world and pay attention. Find beauty in small things and the ordinary. Connect with others, share your ideas with people, and listen to their ideas as well.

How Curiosity Influences People

- **Curiosity Engages Creative Thinking**

Encouraging curiosity creates workplace improvements, such as an increase in creativity. When people are encouraged to rethink organizational processes and goals, they are more creative when performing their tasks than a group that was promoted to be rigid. When faced with a challenge, curiosity encourages individuals to search for solutions. Curiosity breeds innovative thinking, which leads to better decision-making and problem-solving. Encouraging curiosity ignites passion, leading people to take on complex tasks. Curiosity is a powerful influence for seeking new information. Curious people are problem-solvers and see opportunity in every issue, complication, or dilemma. This allows them to make better, more informed decisions as they consistently learn from each obstacle and even seek out new things intentionally.

- **Curiosity Helps Develop Relationships And Improve Communication**

Deep, meaningful relationships do not happen in a vacuum. They require people to be actively curious about others. In a time when mental and emotional health are at the forefront of many employees' minds, helping people connect is crucial. This is only possible by being curious about each other. Curious individuals ask questions and show interest in others' thoughts, experiences, and perspectives, fostering deeper, more meaningful social connections. Curious people are more likely to be open-minded and empathetic—qualities that strengthen relationships. Curiosity is the starting point for learning how to talk to someone and meet them on their level. It allows people to respond to various situations, ideas, and personalities. When leaders engage their teams with curiosity, they can gain information empathetically. Leaders can earn more respect and build trust-filled collaborative relationships by actively listening to and seeking a better understanding of people's struggles. Curiosity leads to open-mindedness because it requires a willingness to consider new ideas and experiences, fostering collaboration among people. Developing strong relationships can also help people broaden their interests. Curious individuals are less likely to adhere to strict beliefs or misconceptions by seeking information and exploring multiple viewpoints.

- **Improves Emotional Well-Being and Resilience**

Curiosity can have a positive impact on mental health by encouraging individuals to engage with the world in a more exploratory way. Curious people often experience feelings of joy and excitement. Following one's curiosity can lead to a sense of fulfillment and purpose, contributing to greater overall happiness and making individuals more resilient in the face of challenges. Curious individuals view challenges as opportunities to learn, grow, and solve problems. Curiosity can significantly shape people's personal development, relationships, and outlook on life, making them more adaptable, motivated, and capable of thriving in a constantly changing world.

Now, we move into the last section: driving action. How do you turn your influence into something tangible?

PART IV:

DRIVING ACTION

LAW 16:

THE FOOT-IN-THE-DOOR TECHNIQUE

The Foot-in-the-Door Technique (FITD) is a remarkable method that starts with a small request to increase the likelihood that a person will agree to a more significant, related request later. The essence of this technique lies in the idea that people are more likely to comply with a more considerable request if they have already agreed to a related smaller one. The Foot-in-the-Door Technique works because people naturally want to keep their actions and attitudes consistent. It's a well-studied strategy in social psychology based on concepts like self-perception and the need for consistency.

The core of FITD is the principle of behavioral consistency, which means people are driven to keep their future actions aligned with past behavior to preserve a steady self-image. When someone agrees to a small request, like signing a petition or completing a quick survey, they view themselves as cooperative or helpful. This change in self-perception, often unconscious, creates a mental commitment to behave in ways that match this new self-image. As a result, when a more significant request comes along, the individual feels compelled to agree, as doing so helps them maintain consistency with the self-image they have just created.

Why does this work effectively? People generally seek to avoid cognitive dissonance—the discomfort that arises when their actions and beliefs are out of alignment. For example, a person who has previously donated to charities is likely to end up as a major volunteer if asked because the initial act of donating subconsciously builds an image of themselves as empathetic and generous. This is how FITD works. It leverages the natural human tendency to justify actions and decisions. Most people's agreement to carry out a request reflects their values as helpful, thoughtful, honorable, and virtuous. This mental correlation often motivates them to act consistently with their internalized values. As a result, they become more likely to accept a related, more significant request when asked later. The psychology behind FITD also highlights how incremental changes in behavior can lead to important shifts in attitudes and decisions.

While FITD is a highly effective tool, it is essential to recognize the potential for misuse in manipulative or unethical ways, even against you. An example familiar to us is how marketing campaigns manipulate consumers into making larger purchases than initially intended or needed. In this chapter, we'll look at a structured exploration and understanding of the FITD technique to gain insight into how to influence behavior effectively and responsibly.

How Small Requests Lead to Bigger Commitments

There's an old saying that the more time, energy, or effort you invest in something, the harder it becomes to walk away. This idea is closely related to the sunk cost fallacy, where people continue investing in a course of action simply because they've already committed resources to it, even if it's no longer the best decision. While the sunk cost fallacy highlights how irrational commitment can be, the psychological mechanisms behind it also explain why small actions often lead to much bigger ones. This principle is at the heart of the Foot-in-the-Door Technique (FITD), where small commitments create psychological momentum that makes individuals more likely to comply with larger requests over time.

The success of FITD is primarily due to its ability to exploit behavioral consistency and self-perception. This perception sets the stage for agreeing to more significant commitments since people are motivated to act in ways that align with their projected self-image. Over time, these small actions create a cycle of consistency, becoming the basis of a person's behavior, attitude, and belief system. The deeper someone invests in their actions, the less likely they are to deviate from the path they've started on.

The Foot-in-the-Door Technique often starts with a minor, low-cost request that feels easy to accept, requires minimal effort, and even less mental power. The simplicity of the initial action makes it less intimidating, thereby reducing resistance. For instance, a request to sign a petition or complete a short survey meets these criteria. These actions seem so trivial that explaining one's refusal to do them would feel like more work than just complying. This seemingly small step influences reactions to more significant asks. Once people agree, they subconsciously see themselves as supportive, cooperative, or helpful.

Our innate desire to act in ways that align with our past behavior, especially when that behavior reflects positively on our self-image, takes care of the rest. This phenomenon is rooted in self-perception theory, which suggests that people develop their attitudes and beliefs based on their actions. For example, a study demon-strated how FITD works with homeowners and requests related to a safe driving campaign. Participants who initially agreed to display a small "Be a Safe Driver" sticker on their windows were significantly more likely to allow the placement of a large billboard on their lawns advocating the same cause. Compliance rates for the second request nearly doubled among those who had first agreed to the smaller one. Such examples also highlight how FITD relates to the Rule of Contrast by demonstrating how smaller commitments create a favorable context for larger requests. Once this perception takes root, subsequent requests feel like logical extensions of who you are.

If you're a manager, you can use this technique by starting with a relatively low-pressure request, such as asking employees to share feedback during a team meeting. Once employees feel com-fortable participating, they are more likely to take on more signif-icant roles, like leading a project or implementing a new strategy. This incremental approach builds confidence and fosters a sense of ownership and involvement, motivating people to stay engaged over the long term.

The FITD technique also employs a kind of cognitive anchoring. Individuals set a mental "anchor" by agreeing to a small request, which influences their future decisions. Each subsequent action feels like a natural step forward rather than a leap into unfa-miliar territory. This incremental, less intimidating approach is persuasive for building up the desired behavior, especially since it allows individuals to gradually adapt their self-image. The initial commitment, however small, becomes the foundation for more significant commitments that ensure people stay consistent with their choices.

Using Gradual Escalation to Influence Behavior

Gradual escalation is an aspect of the Foot-in-the-Door Technique (FITD) that uses incremental steps to influence behavior. This approach makes it easier for individuals to agree to larger, more significant requests as they progress through smaller ones. As previously established, this relies heavily on the principle of behavioral consistency, creating a pathway for sustained engagement so that people can increase their commitment to a cause or task over time.

At the core of gradual escalation is the concept of reducing cognitive load. When individuals are asked to make a significant decision or commitment, the mental effort required can often be overwhelming. Significant obligations, especially those carrying substantial emotional, financial, or social weight, can create resistance and hesitation. By contrast, small requests are easier to agree to because they don't feel as burdensome. When someone is asked to take a small step, it feels less demanding, and the psychological effort required to agree is minimal. This initial, easy commitment creates momentum, making individuals more likely to agree to increasingly significant requests as they have already started down the path. This cumulative process builds psychological commitment that leads to greater involvement over time, even when the final request requires much more resources or effort.

Gradual escalation also reinforces and promotes the self-perception you want to build. As previously established, when individuals agree to requests, they create a shift in their self-image. This change and subsequent reinforcements in self-perception play a critical role in making them more likely to comply with subsequent, more demanding requests. For instance, someone who agrees to share a post for a political campaign may perceive themselves as supportive of the cause. If they continue to share the posts, engage in conversations with like-minded individuals, and participate even passively, they may eventually be drawn into donating their attention, money, or time. They will be more likely to comply because those small steps have subconsciously led them to see themselves as part of the movement, and backing out would feel inconsistent or "off."

This process of gradual escalation is particularly effective in long-term initiatives requiring sustained participation. By reducing or eliminating the typical resistance to significant commitments, especially when they seem to come from "nowhere," this technique ensures that each subsequent step in the commitment circle feels like the logical next move. For example, in customer loyalty programs, businesses often start by offering a free trial or a low-cost initial purchase, followed by more expensive products or services. Similarly, in educational settings, instructors typically introduce simple tasks to help students build understanding, confidence, and commitment before tackling more complex topics. Each action reinforces a sense of accomplishment and increases connection to the task, making it more likely that individuals will continue to engage.

Now that you've learned how to get your foot in the door, it is time to consider loss aversion. In our opening chapter, we discussed the human desire for familiarity and how that relates to an aversion to risk and possible loss. So, how do you push people beyond this fear of loss? We break that down in our next chapter.

LAW 17:

LOSS AVERSION

Loss aversion is rooted in behavioral economics. It describes people's preference to avoid losses over gaining things that would objectively be of the same value. For instance, it explains why a person will avoid a gamble with equal chances to win or lose, even if the potential gain significantly outweighs the loss. Behavioral economists Amos Tversky and Daniel Kahneman coined this concept. The concept stems from the prospect theory, which asserts that people typically feel the pain of loss about twice as much as the pleasure they derive from gaining the same thing, creating an emotional imbalance that significantly affects decision-making. It is also a means to analyze and understand human behaviors across various domains.

Loss aversion is a foundational aspect of human behavior deeply rooted in evolutionary biology and shapes the decisions we make in our day-to-day survival areas, ranging from finances and marketing to relationships and even random choices. For our ancestors, avoiding losses with resources like food, shelter, or social standing was essential for survival. In situations where there was an equal chance of losing or gaining resources, losing could have meant death, and gaining additional resources did not have the same immediate impact or urgency on survival as they preserved their resources instead. Over time, the need to avoid losses became coded into our psychology and passed down through generations. This is a part of our evolutionary process to ensure we survive. Now, it influences how we make decisions for the expected outcomes, even when the stakes are less dire. This bias has a powerful influence on how they respond to risks, incentives, and change.

Loss aversion also interacts with other cognitive biases, such as the endowment effect, which refers to our tendency to value things we already own more highly than things we don't yet possess. Studies have shown that people demand significantly more money to give up an item they own than they would be willing to pay to acquire it. Even during negotiations or conflicts, loss aversion can lead parties to reject objectively favorable offers or hold on to failing businesses simply to avoid the perception of conceding something valuable or taking a loss. This inflated value is linked to the emotional weight we assign to potential losses, even when those losses are relatively minor.

Let's examine this imbalance between losses and gains more closely and why it is crucial to recognize the biases that shape human behavior. Whether applied to marketing strategies that emphasize avoiding losses (e.g., "Don't miss out!") or leadership approaches that frame change in minimizing harm, we will see how and why this approach works.

Why Do People Fear Losing More Than They Value Gaining?

At the heart of loss aversion is a disproportionate emotional reaction to loss compared to gain. Gaining something, such as money, a new opportunity, or a promotion, feels rewarding, but the psychological pain of losing something triggers a much stronger emotional response. Consequently, people are more inclined to avoid losses than pursue equivalent gains. Cognitive psychology provides insight into this phenomenon. The human brain is wired so that when we experience a loss, our brains process the information rapidly, leading to heightened activity in the amygdala, the region responsible for fear and emotional responses. This activation creates a visceral, immediate emotional response to loss, causing us to grieve our losses longer. In contrast, gains tend to activate the brain's reward system, the ventral striatum, but the emotional response is less intense. This imbalance means that the experience of loss is far more painful, impactful, and long-lasting than the pleasure derived from gaining something, even if it is of equal value.

Cognitive biases further shape how we perceive losses and gains. Humans are inherently risk-averse, meaning we often focus on the fear of losing something before considering how the potential satisfaction of gaining something new outweighs the loss. This risk aversion typically leads people to make conservative choices in hopes of avoiding actions that could result in loss, despite the potential rewards. Studies show that individuals are more likely to hold onto losing investments, such as stocks, rather than sell them and accept a loss. The emotional discomfort of recognizing a financial, social, or personal loss can overpower rational thought unless one is aware of it. Investors may convince themselves that the value will rebound and cling to the hope of reversing their loss, even when evidence suggests that selling and moving on would lead to better outcomes. Market experts often become desensitized to this, quickly selling out and shifting to the next opportunity when data dictates.

This tendency to avoid loss extends beyond professional life. In personal relationships, many people cling to bad situations because they fear losing love, security, or social status. The anticipated emotional pain and uncertainty of a potential breakup, job change, or loss of status can feel so overwhelming that individuals avoid taking necessary steps to improve their situations.

Another fascinating manifestation of loss aversion is the "endowment effect," which occurs when individuals assign a higher value to things they own simply because they own them. This psychological attachment to an object, idea, or opportunity makes the thought of losing it more distressing. People often overvalue what they have because the potential loss feels psychologically painful. This effect influences behavior in financial and social decisions. For instance, someone may avoid selling an underperforming stock they've owned for years due to their attachment to it. Similarly, individuals may resist giving up a bad habit that negatively impacts their well-being because they do not want to lose the comfort of familiarity associated with that habit, even when adopting a healthier lifestyle offers similar comforts with better advantages.

Framing Decisions to Highlight Potential Loss

As much as loss aversion affects human internal psychological biases, it also holds sway in how external forces shape our decisions by framing information. For instance, studies have shown that people are more likely to act when they perceive potential losses because losses trigger stronger emotional responses. Marketers, politicians, religious bodies, and decision-makers have used this knowledge to their advantage for longer than the phenomenon has had a name. You will often find them framing situations in ways that highlight what the people who need them stand to lose rather than focusing on what they might gain. In doing so, they tap into the deep, primal fear of loss that they know will often override rational thinking and use it to drive the behavior they would like.

This framing effect is particularly effective when it comes to consumer behavior. Marketers are adept at leveraging loss aversion and the psychological concept of "FOMO" (fear of missing out) to motivate purchases by emphasizing what consumers might lose if they don't act quickly. Specific popular phrases build a consumer's sense of urgency and encourage them to make quicker, ill-thought-out decisions. Advertisers frequently frame limited-time offers with phrases implying that a failure to act will result in the loss of an opportunity. Sometimes, the product itself might not be something you need or of great value. The deal they are advertising might not even be as extraordinary as presented. However, the fear of losing the opportunity is a strong motivator that drives people to act impulsively.

Politicians also use the loss aversion effect. More often than not, campaigns will emphasize what voters stand to lose rather than what they stand to gain. Politicians and advocacy groups will spend more time framing a policy or candidate's platform regarding potential losses, such as the erosion of personal freedoms, financial security, or social status. These campaigns use people's fears as motivators that push them to take action to protect their perceived security. These actions are often for the benefit of the person instigating the fear. They will usually use the fear of losing one's rights, privileges, or identity as a potent motivator to deride rationality and influence voting behavior and public opinion.

Loss aversion can also influence decision-making abilities in personal relationships and life choices. For centuries, people have remained in unhealthy relationships or avoided career changes out of fear of losing stability, even if the potential for improvement is evident. The way most people see it, the discomfort and perceived uncertainty that arise from losing a long-term partner, a familiar routine, or social standing can outweigh the possible benefits of change. This fear of losing what we already have often leads to remaining in harmful situations instead of risking the unknown.

When you understand the mechanics of loss aversion, you unlock significant value for yourself in your decision-making process. Recognizing how framing can influence perceptions of loss and gain makes you better equipped to make more informed choices, even when faced with tough decisions. You can also protect yourself from marketing schemes and propaganda of all kinds. Furthermore, you'll better overcome the instinct to pull away from risks. You can then train your mind to understand how to take calculated risks and reframe challenges. Because of how integral it is to the human psyche, the fear of losing something will almost always cloud your judgment. However, do the work to consciously reframe the situation to highlight the potential benefits you stand to gain instead of the loss. You can free yourself from the crippling fear of loss and focus on the possibilities of improvement available to you. This reframing will rewire your brain to embrace change as a part of your growth process and navigate uncertainty with a clearer, more value-driven perspective.

You might be deciding whether to purchase, contemplating a political choice, or weighing a personal decision. Remember that highlighting the risks of loss can increase your motivation to act, often not to your benefit. Framing our choice consequences as positive or negative affects how we evaluate potential outcomes. Reframing situations to emphasize the potential for gain can help you overcome the paralysis that comes from the fear of losing. Both perspectives, loss and gain, are critical in shaping behavior, and understanding the psychology behind loss aversion allows individuals and organizations to make more rational, goal-oriented decisions.

LAW 18:

THE AUTHORITY EFFECT

The Authority Effect explains why we tend to trust and follow individuals we regard as experts, leaders, or figures of power. From our interactions with doctors, teachers, and managers to political leaders or even social media influencers we follow, the presence of authority influences nearly every decision we make. Understanding the Authority Effect helps us comprehend why we easily trust authority figures and why we sometimes make or accept decisions based on their whims without questioning them.

Like the loss aversion effect, the Authority Effect can also be traced to our evolutionary history. Early humans had to depend on the guidance of those with more knowledge and experience to survive. This person could have been an elder who knew how to forage for non-poisonous food or a leader who could navigate conflict. The more closely they adhered to these authorities, the better their chances were of staying safe and thriving as a community. This instinct to defer to those in charge now forms part of our pathological awareness as a survival mechanism and our social conditioning. Humans have only started to question authority in recent years, and they do so only when the authority figure has shown beyond doubt that they are incapable of leading as they should. As a result, we still follow the lead of those we perceive as experts or authority figures with little hesitation.

Now, authority figures are everywhere. We've also learned to recognize them through social cues like uniforms, titles, or credentials, such as seeing a doctor in a white coat or a CEO in a tailored suit. These symbols of authority instantly tell us to listen and trust their expertise and often prevent us from evaluating whether they're genuinely trustworthy or competent. We simply assume and trust that they are based on the cues with which we were socialized. This isn't necessarily bad since it helps us make decisions quickly, especially when we don't have time to analyze everything. After all, it's more efficient to trust a doctor when we require medical care or a leader when we're working on a team project.

The Authority Effect can be a strong tool to push society forward, but, like all tools, it can also be used manipulatively. When you become aware of how authority in your field can influence your actions, you can make more informed decisions and challenge bad practices as they arise. Here, we'll explore how we can balance trust in figures who objectively know better than we do with critical thinking. The goal isn't to reject authority but to understand how to respond to or use it wisely and responsibly.

How Perceived Expertise Boosts Influence

One of the most effective ways to influence the behavior of others is to appear confident, charismatic, and all-knowing. When you seem knowledgeable or qualified in a specific field, particularly one where your audience is not very experienced, they are likelier to trust your advice, follow your guidance, and defer to your decisions, even when their instincts might urge caution. The Authority Effect is more potent when you boost your credibility through credentials, attire, demeanor, or societal reputation. This means that you don't necessarily need all the credentials to exude the aura of expertise, which is so strong that even minor cues can subtly shift behavior. To a large extent, this is why experts in their fields come across as authority figures and can influence other people's decisions. Unsurprisingly, history has shown us that this unquestioning trust can lead to surprising and sometimes harmful outcomes.

An example is the popular obedience experiments conducted to understand how far ordinary people could go in committing morally questionable acts simply because an authority figure told them to do so. The study was created by Stanley Milgram, a psychologist, in the 1960s. He led participants to believe they were dispensing increasingly severe electric shocks to a strapped person. Unbeknownst to them, this person was an actor and was never actually harmed. They labeled the shocks from mild to "dangerous" levels. They saw a researcher wearing a lab coat as a symbol of expertise and authority, especially at that time, calmly and confidently instructing participants to continue, even as the supposed recipient of the shocks expressed distress or pleaded for the process to stop.

Many participants obeyed the authority figure, continuing to administer shocks far beyond their comfort levels. The experiment participants looked at the researcher and the symbols of his perceived expertise—the lab coat, the formal environment, and the scientific language—and decided these were enough to make them override their moral instincts and sense of empathy. This tells us something troubling: the average person's belief in an expert can cause them to let go of their critical judgment and prioritize obedience over ethical considerations.

The power of perceived expertise shapes our everyday lives in visible and subtle ways. We would immediately consider a doctor wearing a white coat credible until their actions breed suspicion. Patients willingly accept treatment plans or prescriptions with minimal questioning because they assume the doctor's expertise is valid and trustworthy. In financial services, clients are more willing to follow advice from professionals with impressive titles like "financial advisor" or "investment strategist," even if the recommendations are risky or flawed. Research shows that people will follow the instructions of a person wearing a uniform, such as a security guard, rather than one in casual clothing. It doesn't matter if the person in casual clothing relays more logical instructions because they focus more on what the uniform stands for. The uniform, in their minds, becomes a shortcut to trust, signaling competence and authority. This reliance on superficial markers is rooted in cognitive efficiency. Because our brains are wired to take mental shortcuts to save time and effort, social conditioning uses this advantage to ensure we follow and prioritize obedience as a quick fix. Instead of carefully evaluating an individual's knowledge or competence, we look for quick signals—like titles, attire, or reputation—to determine whether they deserve our trust.

Understanding how perceived expertise influences behavior is one way to break out of this cycle, take charge of our lives, and make more discerning and thoughtful decisions. Awareness of this phenomenon allows us to engage with authority figures in a way that encourages critical thinking and builds valid trust and belief.

Ways to Establish Credibility Quickly

Building credibility quickly is essential to earning trust and influencing others, whether professionally or personally. You might be pitching an idea, rallying support for a cause, or trying to be taken seriously on a project. In all these cases, appearing to have the expertise to carry out what is needed can make all the difference. However, perceived expertise can be a double-edged sword. While it can build trust and simplify decisions, it can also be misused. The real challenge ahead of you is establishing credibility quickly and effectively, especially when you don't have the time or reputation to back you up. To succeed at this ethically and positively, you must understand the key ways people and organizations can convey trustworthiness.

1. Visual Cues as Symbols of Authority

One fast way to establish credibility is through visual cues that signal expertise. There is an idiom based on how people dress because humans instinctively respond to visual symbols of authority, like uniforms, formal attire, or professional accessories. These cues act as shortcuts for evaluating competence. In corporate settings, dressing in business attire, wearing a name badge, or displaying certifications achieves a similar effect. As we have learned, these visual markers do not guarantee competence. Look around at the people who seem to command the most respect in the field you want to break into and recreate the ways they visually create the perception of credibility.

2. Confident Communication

Language and communication skills are crucial when attempting to establish expertise quickly. Since people naturally trust individuals who speak concisely and confidently, you can learn to discuss your topic this way. Using appropriate terminology can demonstrate knowledge, but learning to strike a balance is also essential. Overloading a conversation with jargon risks alienating listeners, while explaining complex ideas in relatable terms signals mastery. Research shows that confidence and clear articulation can make you seem warm and influence trust. Listeners often associate confidence with competence, especially when they lack the expertise to verify the content.

3. Borrowed Credibility Through Associations

You can improve your credibility through association with trusted individuals, brands, or institutions—a concept known as borrowed credibility. For example, a product endorsed by a reputable scientist, a leader featured in a respected publication, or a professional who has worked with notable organizations benefits from the trust people place in those entities. Because borrowed credibility provides a shortcut to influence, especially in competitive environments where standing out is essential, it is also the easiest tool for exploitation and manipulation. Be mindful of this. The appearance of expertise is easy to create, but going too far can be risky.

4. The Surprising Role of Transparency

Transparency is a sneaky way to build credibility. Openly recognizing and acknowledging your limitations, challenges, or uncertainties makes you relatable. Everyone has struggled with the downsides of a great idea, so they're more likely to believe in you if you're upfront about yours. It shows that you understand your idea or vision's shortcomings and are working on fixing them. This is a key ingredient in building trust. However, note that this relies heavily on how you phrase your language. If done poorly, you can come across as incompetent. For example, a doctor who explains the risks and benefits of a treatment plan instead of simply rattling off the risks will seem more competent and trustworthy. Similarly, leaders who admit mistakes and share lessons learned gain more respect than those who project an air of perfection. This works because, in an age where the pressure for perfection is ever-increasing while distrust remains rampant, authenticity and humility stand out as valid indicators of genuine expertise.

In all of this, you need to balance these ways out with substance. To establish credibility ethically and effectively, you must ensure that your expertise is, on some level, both verifiable and authentic. These strategies build trust quickly and foster lasting influence when backed by genuine competence. The Authority Effect is undeniably compelling, but when credibility and trust are earned through demonstrated expertise, you become a long-lasting force while maintaining relevance.

LAW 19:

THE POWER OF STORIES

Humans have been telling stories for thousands of years. The art of storytelling existed long before the invention of writing or the development of modern technology. From prehistoric cave paintings to bedtime tales, stories have been fundamental to communicating, connecting, and making sense of the world. The power of storytelling is both a cultural and psychological phenomenon. Multiple studies have shown that the human brain is wired to respond to narratives far more deeply than to facts, statistics, or logic. While data speaks to our rational mind, stories tap into our emotions, creating vivid experiences that engage, persuade, and inspire.

Stories enable us to capture attention by framing information in relatable and compelling ways. They activate multiple areas of the brain—not just the language-processing regions but also those involved in sensory experience, emotion, and decision-making. As a result, stories have the unique power to make abstract ideas concrete, connect individuals across time and space, and move people toward action in ways that mere logic often cannot. Stories have always been at the heart of leadership and social movements. Martin Luther King Jr.'s "I Have a Dream" speech remains iconic because of how well it offers insights into racial inequality by painting a vivid, aspirational vision of the world he would love to see. His shared story of freedom, equality, and unity still resonates deeply with people's values and emotions. It continues to serve as a source of inspiration for modern leaders who wish to make history.

The same holds true in marketing. Companies don't just sell products; they tell stories about how those products can solve problems, improve lives, or fulfill dreams. Think of Apple's call to "think differently" or Nike's narratives of perseverance and achievement. When appropriately crafted, these stories are designed to inform while engaging your emotions. The aim is to inspire you to take action and build loyalty to the brand in subtle ways that stick with you.

What makes stories so powerful? They provide meaning. Humans crave structure and coherence in a chaotic world; stories give us just that. They help us understand causes and consequences. They also help us build empathy by allowing us to put ourselves in someone else's shoes and visualize what we could have done and the outcomes of our decisions. This psychological power is why storytelling is a cornerstone of education, politics, advertising, and leadership.

Why Do We Respond to Narratives?

Humans are both storytellers and story consumers. Long before written language existed, our ancestors shared knowledge, traditions, and survival strategies through oral stories. This wasn't just for entertainment; it was critical for passing down vital information in ways that were easy to remember and act upon. Today, while the mediums have evolved, the fundamental connection between humans and stories remains the same. Narratives are not just something we enjoy; they are how we make sense of the world, our experiences, and each other.

As social creatures, we are wired to seek patterns and meaning in our daily interactions to understand our place in the world. Stories are our way of finding structure and making sense of the complex information we learn daily. They break information into a clear narrative arc with a beginning, middle, and end that our brains can easily comprehend and internalize. This works exceptionally well because this structure mimics our own life experiences. Events unfold, obstacles appear, and we find resolutions. This helps us understand information more efficiently, as it allows us to project our thoughts, struggles, and potential outcomes onto characters and view them holistically. A well-crafted story brings information to life in a way that purely factual communication cannot, making it more relatable and memorable.

In the introductory part of this chapter, we mentioned that stories activate multiple brain regions. These regions include those responsible for sensory processing, emotions, and even motor functions. This phenomenon is known as neural coupling. This is why an immersive story makes us feel like we're living the story ourselves. You could be reading a book about someone running through a dense forest. The text doesn't just remain words; we can "feel" and visualize the crunch of leaves and the thrill or fear the character experiences at that moment. This deep mental engagement makes stories more memorable and impactful than facts, as they transform information into experiences. This emotional engagement plays a key role in why stories resonate so strongly. Research shows that it becomes far easier to remember and act upon information that triggers emotions—such as joy, fear, or empathy. For instance, a personal story about an individual's hardship will leave a lasting impression, whereas statistics alone might not.

Additionally, shared stories help create healthy bonds. They bring people together because they make us feel seen and understood, building the belief that we are part of something bigger than ourselves. By sharing narratives, we build connections, strengthen trust, and create a sense of belonging that holds communities together. Stories unite people by creating a sense of shared experience and building a common identity across generations or within social circles. This could be the story of a cultural tradition, a company's founding, or a political leader's journey. These narratives are curated to resonate with others and align them with collective values and goals.

Crafting Compelling Stories to Inspire Action

Stories are some of the best ways to communicate with and reach out to others. Fortunately, it's a skill you can work on, polish, and improve with practice. It is even better when you find ways to include statistics and data that inform your audience while building a world with your words to connect with their emotions, values, and imaginations. A compelling narrative should connect us to meaning by bridging the gap between access to information and taking action by transforming ideas, thoughts, and visions into something vivid, relatable, and tangible.

A story shouldn't just explain what to do; it should also show the why of it and the consequences attached. It should allow people to see themselves in the narrative and imagine the change they can effect. Here are key elements you should consider when crafting your imaginary world:

1. A Hook to Capture Attention

If you aim to trap someone in the world you are building, you can't afford a shabby opening. People don't gather around campfires for dull stories; they sleep off halfway when forced to. A compelling story should begin with an engaging hook to grab and hold the audience's attention. Instead of starting with dry facts, drop them into the middle of something they can't ignore. Create curiosity or emotional connection right away. When next you craft a story for impact, consider opening with a specific scenario that engages the audience and forces their attention to you. This could be a relatable problem, a surprising fact, or an emotional moment that resonates with the listener's experiences.

2. Focus on Conflict, Stakes, and Resolution

Nobody wants to hear a story that is all joy and light. There's no fun or lesson in that. The heart of any great story lies in its conflict. Because conflict creates tension that holds the audience's attention, ensuring they stay engaged, you need to have these questions in mind when crafting your story:

What challenges are you facing? What's at stake if you don't resolve it?

Your story could be about a small bakery owner fighting to keep her business afloat or a community standing up against a corporation threatening their water supply. A protagonist who struggles to achieve a goal naturally inspires action because it mirrors real-life struggles. The higher the character's stakes, the more compelling your story is. This is how you're able to craft stories that influence others. Always ensure that your story has a clear structure:

The Setup

The Challenge

The Resolution

By showing how you overcome a challenge, the story delivers an arc of struggle and triumph that leaves people thinking, if they can do it, so can I. The aim is to Inspire them to see themselves as characters who face the challenges you need them to connect emotionally to and come out stronger. People are far more motivated to act when they see proof of progress or transformation.

3. **Make It Personal and Authentic**

Can you count the times you've rolled your eyes or laughed at a commercial because you thought, "No way they expect me to believe that?" While this is a form of marketing, it's a terrible way to tell a story. Audiences connect deeply with real and honest narratives because they tap into shared emotions and experiences. If your story doesn't feel real, it will fall flat—not in a funny, campy way.

To ground your narrative in reality, use personal anecdotes, testimonials, or real-world examples. People want to see themselves reflected in the story, so avoid overly polished or generic tales. Instead, highlight emotions like vulnerability, resilience, or triumph, which evoke empathy and inspire others to believe they can take similar actions.

Authenticity is your best friend. Share small, vivid details that bring your story to life. You could say, "We helped farmers increase crop yields," or you could say, "With the new irrigation system, Aisha grew enough tomatoes to feed her family and sell at the market, sending her kids to school for the first time." People may not remember your farmers and crop yields, but they will remember Aisha's tomatoes, how they sent her kids to school, and your role in that story.

4. End with a Clear Call to Action

Stories can transform passive listeners into motivated actors by combining emotional resonance, conflict, authenticity, and a call to action. Even when your story serves entertainment purposes, you still need to leave your audience with something they can hold on to—a story without a clear purpose or follow-up steps risks being forgotten. If you want to inspire action, you need to lead people somewhere. After the story, people will think, "So, what now?" Your call to action acts as the final destination, but it must feel like the natural next step, not a hard sell.

For instance, if you've just shared a story about how dona-
tions helped build a medical center for internally displaced
persons (IDPs), you don't want to abruptly say, "Give us
money." This would break your connection with the audience and diminish the emotional high of your story. Instead, consider something like, "Your $20 today could help
a mother survive tomorrow." This approach connects their
action to the story's resolution in a tangible, emotionally
satisfying way, making them feel like they're the missing
piece in the puzzle.

This will feel like a lot, but you already have a cognitive understanding of how to do most of this. You understand the primacy
effect of law 9, so setting the right tone is a breeze. With the loss
aversion effect, you know how to maximize the stakes in your
story by highlighting what's at risk if no action is taken. People are
naturally wired to pay more attention when they sense a potential
loss, so weaving that into your narrative keeps your audience
hooked.

LAW 20:

THE COMMITMENT BIAS

While discussing the Foot-in-the-Door (FITD) technique, we high-lighted how humans have a deep-seated need to see themselves as consistent. Once someone commits to an idea, takes a stance, or aligns themselves with a particular course of action, they are remarkably likely to stick to it until significantly convinced other-wise. This tendency, known as commitment bias, effectively drives behavior and shapes many of our decisions, from everyday choic-es to monumental life events.

Consider how often you have agreed to help with an additional task after completing one, feeling obligated to assist. People of-ten attribute this to guilt; however, it often relates more to their self-perception. If you can convince someone that they are the type of person who helps others, you activate their commitment bias. When they complete tasks and follow through, they begin to form a part of their identity around that behavior. For example, when someone agrees to even a small request—like saying, "Yes, I'll help with that" or "Sure, I'll support this cause"—they start to see themselves through the lens of that commitment. Their actions create a mental framework: "I'm someone who cares about this; I'm the type of person who follows through."

The commitment bias amplifies the FITD effect, as people naturally seek to align their future actions with their past behaviors. When they say "yes" to a new, related request, it's because they recognize the belief that supporting this cause is "who they are." This drive to ensure our actions align with our beliefs helps keep promises, advance projects, and foster relationships. You've likely seen the consequences when there's a disconnect between a person's actions and their statements.

Understanding the interplay between commitment and consistency reveals why seemingly small, inconsequential actions can lead to profound changes over time. For instance, a neighbor who says, "Sure, I'll come to the community meeting," is far more likely to become actively involved in local projects than someone who never made that initial commitment.

The commitment bias functions similarly to the primacy effect and the law of social proof, as it taps into our fundamental need to view ourselves as coherent and reliable. You can leverage these principles to inspire collaboration, foster trust, and encourage productive action. By the end of this chapter, you'll understand how the commitment bias operates and how it complements strategies like the FITD technique.

Getting People to Stay Consistent With Their Public Promises

With how social media and digital connections have grown, our actions have become more visible than ever, and holding someone to their public promise has gotten easier. When people make their promises known to others, the stakes get higher because there's something about making a commitment in front of others that increases the pressure to follow through. They're now accountable to themselves, their social circle, peers, or even a broader audience. In today's world, influencers and brands often announce initiatives with fanfare and get their followers involved for a reason. It's to want to appear reliable and trustworthy, especially when the world seems to be watching.

The psychology behind public commitments has much to do with cognitive dissonance—an uncomfortable tension between their actions and words if they fail to follow through. People are highly motivated to act according to what they've said to avoid judgment from others and protect their sense of self. But how do you use this to encourage genuine follow-through?

1. **Using Social Proof to Reinforce Commitment and Make it Meaningful**

People will stick with their promises if they know others are doing the same. Social proof can be a helpful motivator, showing people their peers and the wider community expect them to follow through. Knowing this allows you to tap into the social pressure people feel to align with the group so you can increase their commitment to the task. You can also take it a step further and encourage commitments to be made genuinely. One great way to do this is by starting with a small task like asking them to share their goals during a meeting, writing them down in a public forum, and then assigning a commitment to them based on these goals. That way, it feels more natural to agree to it, especially since they've previously agreed to a related task. For instance, someone who cares deeply about their community might be more motivated to follow through on a public promise if it's tied to positively impacting others. Learning how to build up momentum, which you can leverage later on, is essential.

2. **Anchor It to Their Identity**

This connects directly to the Commitment Bias. People want their actions to reflect who they believe they are, so when you get someone to commit to a course of action publicly, you're not just asking them to fulfill a task—you're shaping how they see themselves. If you can tie their promise to a personal value or identity, they'll feel a more substantial need to stick with it. For example, instead of saying, "Would you donate to this cause?" you might say, "As someone who values education, would you be willing to support this program?" Once they publicly affirm that identity, their actions are more likely to follow suit. People will work much harder to keep their word when they feel that doing so aligns with who they believe they are or want to become.

3. **Leverage the Power of Social Accountability**

The simplest way to ensure someone stays consistent with their promise is to get them to say it out loud or post it where others can see it. When people know others are aware of their commitments, it adds an extra layer of accountability. The act of public commitment makes it psychologically harder for people to back out later on.

Group settings are particularly effective for this. Consider workplace environments where team members set goals in front of their peers. They're far more likely to meet those goals because failing them feels like letting the group down. The same logic applies to personal relationships—if someone promises a friend they'll attend an event or complete a project, they're less likely to back out.

4. Create Incremental Opportunities to Act

It's one thing to make a public promise but another to sustain it. Here, you can use the FITD technique to break the commitment into smaller, manageable steps and celebrate each milestone. Allowing people to take small, visible actions in line with their promises effectively keeps them on track. If someone pledges to volunteer more in the future and you want to hold them to it, start with an easy, one-time event before encouraging ongoing participation. This builds momentum and reinforces their sense of consistency over time. This method fosters consistency by allowing people to show that they're living up to their word while building and creating in their minds what will make them more likely to take on more significant tasks.

Even though public commitments are robust, the fine line between healthy accountability and coercion is thin. To get the maximum results, you need people to feel ownership over their promises rather than be forced into them. It is, therefore, of great importance that you create an environment where they want to follow through because it aligns with their values and identity, not because they feel cornered, obligated, or guilt-tripped into it. The public promises you hold people to should constantly strengthen individual resolve while serving as a way to influence those watching from the sidelines. Seeing someone else sticking to their word inspires trust, credibility, and a ripple effect of influence.

How to use subtle cues to secure agreement

Sometimes, you will find yourself in a situation where overt promises or grand declarations won't work, and you must use subtlety. Here, you can use trim, almost imperceptible cues to guide the person toward agreement without them realizing the psychological forces at play. You can call this the "subtle art of planting seeds." This is when you create situations where people feel like they're making independent decisions, even though their behavior is being influenced.

This is another situation that blends well with the FITD technique. Building upon small, seemingly simple suggestions and agreements creates the groundwork for more significant commitments later. In practice, the initial ask and suggestion rely heavily on how you present them for them to work. Subtle cues should amplify the likelihood of that first "yes" and lay a solid foundation for long-term consistency. How do you do this? Read carefully:

1. **Start with Small, Manageable Requests**

   In the previous chapters, we've established that people naturally hesitate to jump into significant commitments without context or trust. To overcome this, start small. The magic lies in the psychology of small agreements: once someone says "yes" to something minor, they're much more likely to say "yes" to more significant asks in the future. Subtlety can help you build up an initial ask that feels natural and unpressured. It's always best to frame the initial ask as a no-big-deal favor or a friendly suggestion rather than a commitment after dropping subtle hints about its importance or value.

2. **Use Body Language and Tone to Reinforce the Agreement**

In much the same way actions speak louder than words, nonverbal cues reach your audience faster than your words do. It tells them how to receive and respond to your message and lets them know what you think about your message. A warm tone of voice, a reassuring smile, or an open posture all encourage agreement. When next you're asking someone to commit, try nodding as you pose the question. This acts as a subconscious prompt to the other person to nod. In this way, you make the person mirror your actions. This helps establish rapport and makes it easier for someone to agree without feeling coerced. We discussed this in depth in Law 4.

Similarly, using inclusive language like "we" or "us" creates a sense of collaboration. Phrases like "We can get started with just a quick step" or "Let's take a small action to see where it leads" subtly imply partnership, making the ask feel more approachable and less transactional.

3. **Anchor the Request in Their Values or Identity**

A huge part of influencing people is finding where their

values lie and reflecting those values to them. People are far more likely to commit when the request aligns with their values or identity. Subtly weaving these connections into your conversations can make a world of difference. For instance, if someone identifies as environmentally conscious, you might frame a small commitment to reflect their concern for the planet.

This strategy plays on the commitment bias by linking the act of agreement to how they see themselves. Once they take that small step, they'll feel compelled to stay consistent with your reinforced identity. Over time, this builds a more profound sense of ownership over their actions, making more extensive commitments feel natural.

4. Use Open-Ended Questions to Lead the Way

Open-ended questions encourage people to think deeply about their ideas and values. They actively invite them to internalize the commitment while opening the door for an initial ask, making them feel like they are part of the decision-making process.

You also have the advantage of making them believe the decision is entirely theirs, mainly when you use questions like these. When your audience can think about what they were asked, they also get the space to internalize it. This is an effective way to leverage their reasoning and secure agreement without overt persuasion subtly. The beauty of this approach is that it avoids resistance while encouraging buy-in at a deeper level.

5. **Offer Social Proof, But Keep It Low-Key**

Subtle social proof can also nudge people toward agreement. Mentioning how others have already committed or pointing out a growing trend can gently encourage someone to say "yes." For instance, you might say, "A lot of people have been interested in this idea lately," or "This approach has worked well for others in your situation." The key is to avoid overloading the conversation with evidence or making the other person feel like you're selling them on something. Subtle social proof works best when it feels incidental rather than deliberate.

The aim, with subtle cues, should not be to force agreement but to create and encourage an environment where agreement feels natural and easy. If you factor in the commitment bias when guiding people in a particular direction, you can ensure that the small moments of agreement create a chain reaction. At this point, each "yes" builds up a landing pad for the next one.

As a person seeking to influence others, you should try different ways to secure support for a new project, foster collaboration, or influence everyday decisions. However, subtlety is one of the best tools to increase your reach and boost your charisma. Nobody likes an overbearing, loud person. Remember that this should, first and foremost, always be about understanding people's thoughts and using that insight to make the commitment process effortless. When done well, this approach leaves people agreeing with you and feeling genuinely good about their choice.

LAW 21:

THE EMOTION-LOGIC BALANCE

Despite popular opinion about whether it is emotional and which is logical, neuroscientist Antonio Damasio's research reveals that the human decision-making process is neither purely rational nor entirely emotional. A secret third element exists at the intersection of these two forces. The combination of emotion and logic shapes our every choice. At every point in your decision-making process, whether for mundane daily chores or life-altering commitments, you first consider how it makes you feel and then the facts of the situation. Sure, logic provides structure and justification, while emotion drives urgency and gives meaning. However, when they work well together, they become an effective tool for persuasion and influence. Finding the right balance between them will make all the difference in how well you can influence others to create your preferred outcome.

Psychology shows just how crucial this balance is. In the 1990s, Damasio's research revealed that our emotions are deeply inter-twined with, and essential to, our decision-making processes. Despite how much people like to pride themselves on being logical, individuals with damaged emotional centers in their brains struggle to make even simple decisions despite retaining full cognitive function. These findings emphasize that while logic processes information, emotion prioritizes it. In essence, emotions give life to facts. They turn abstract ideas and thoughts into actionable decisions. This interplay is at the heart of influencing behavior. Earlier chapters in this book, like those on the Framing Effect and Commitment Bias, have shown how certain psychological principles use either emotion or logic to shape our actions. The Emotion-Logic Balance builds on these principles by examining how the dual appeal of feelings and reason can amplify persuasive efforts.

This balance is critical when trust, motivation, or buy-in is required. For instance, leaders who frame messages with emotional resonance are likely to inspire loyalty, but without logical reinforcement, their ideas may lack credibility. Similarly, marketers who use only emotional triggers like fear or desire can come off as manipulative if they do not back up their claims with logic.

Many believe that decisions should be driven purely by cold, calculated reasoning. However, reality is far more nuanced and complex. People naturally lean on emotions as shortcuts to make complex choices quickly. This reliance on emotion is a survival mechanism that enables faster and more adaptive decisions in uncertain situations.

Emotion engages; logic reassures. Statistics and evidence build a foundation for a heartfelt story that draws in people and solidifies their beliefs. An argument rooted solely in logic will fail to resonate with your audience because it lacks the emotional chord that compels people to act. This principle explains why political campaigns, marketing strategies, and interpersonal negotiations often integrate emotive storytelling with rational appeals to create maximum impact.

Combining Emotional Appeal with Logical Reasoning

To make the most effective decisions and influence others to do the same, you have to understand the related facts and the impact each of them will have on the people around you. Again, humans are social creatures. How we see the world, both naturally and through societal conditioning, rests on our five senses and our "sixth sense." Emotion provides the impulse to act, and logic offers the justification that makes that action seem sensible.

Studies show that the human brain processes and responds to emotional stimuli faster than logical stimuli, helping us make quick, instinctive decisions, especially in urgent situations. However, emotions alone can sometimes be dangerous, just as logic alone can quickly create more problems. Purely emotional decisions might be impulsive or reactive, while the allure of using logic alone is to be detached from the situation and appear unbiased. Logic can provide short-term efficient solutions but often lacks empathy, making a solution less long-lasting and acceptable. It can also oversimplify complex issues, leading to resolutions that act like a blanket rather than an actual solution. Finding a balance between the two is essential because purely emotional decisions may be impulsive or reactive, and strictly logical decisions rarely find applications outside the blueprint problem. When faced with complex choices, it is best to seek logical explanations to confirm or clarify your emotional responses. How do you combine the two in your role as a thought leader?

Firstly, you can use emotions to grab and hold your audience's attention. For this to be successful, you must create a personal connection between you and your audience by using emotions to make your message visually tangible and morally relatable. Tell a compelling story, use vivid imagery, or share an anecdotal joke to evoke feelings and draw people in. Once you have established the emotional connection, back it up with logical arguments. Presenting facts, statistics, and data provides a solid foundation for emotional appeals and builds the trust your audience has in you. This combination ensures that the message is engaging, credible, and well-supported. It also positions you as an authority figure. Amidst this, ensure you balance emotional appeal with logical reasoning throughout the communication process. Keep track of which areas to engage people with their minds or hearts so you can maintain audience engagement while continuously reinforcing the message's validity.

One of the best ways to get your audience to trust you and become more receptive to your message is by showing that you understand their feelings and perspectives. Doing this makes you appear authentic, which, in turn, makes your message more relatable to them. To increase your chances of being persuasive, take it a step further by acknowledging some of their direct concerns during your message and providing your solutions in a thoughtful manner. Finally, simplify complex information into easily digestible chunks. Assume you have an audience ranging from age 5 to 60 and must connect with them using one message. You neither have the time nor resources to create different messages that resonate with each generation. Your message must be universal but also nuanced. Use emotional and logical elements to break down intricate topics, making them more accessible and understandable. This is particularly important now because one moment, you're speaking to a room of people; the next moment, you're viral, and more people are nodding along to what you've said.

This approach ensures you can expand your reach while carrying your audience along when the opportunity arises.

Tailoring Your Message to Resonate with Diverse Audiences

Being an effective communicator requires you to deliver a well-constructed argument that demonstrates a nuanced understanding of how diverse audiences will perceive and process the information you share with them. Research in psychology consistently underscores that individuals interpret messages through the lens of their unique experiences, values, and cognitive frameworks. Adapting your message involves tailoring communication to align with these factors. This enhances the clarity of the message and its persuasive power. Adapting a message should not compromise its integrity; the core idea should remain intact even if you adjust its framing.

The importance of framing in communication has been extensively discussed in Law 14. It demonstrates how the presentation of information—whether in terms of gains or losses—can significantly influence decision-making. For example, a medical treatment described as having a "90% survival rate" is more likely to be favored than one described as having a "10% mortality rate," even though the two statements convey identical information. The loss aversion effect explains why this works: highlighting how you frame information matters as much as the information you convey. Taking all of these factors into consideration is what helps you build an audience-centric message.

This communication style takes advantage of how people interpret facts through the lens of their specific cultural values and environment. This is why adapting your message to your audience is essential. Studies have shown that people are more likely to accept scientific evidence if it fits their preconceived cultural views.

Here are some ways to adapt your message effectively:

1. **Know Your Audience:**

   Research based on consumer psychology indicates that marketing campaigns are more effective when they align with the cultural or social identity of the target group (Aaker et al., 2001). Developing an understanding of your audience's demographics, values, and cognitive styles is the best way to create a message that is relatable enough to influence. A study by Han and Shavitt found that individualistic appeals (e.g., "Stand out from the crowd") work better in Western cultures, whereas collectivistic appeals (e.g., "Support your community") resonate more in East Asian cultures. Knowing whether the bulk of your audience is academically inclined and would prefer detailed, evidence-based arguments or family-oriented and would appreciate emotionally resonant narratives can shape how you craft your message. A tech-based audience might respond more favorably to logical reasoning with light banter. In contrast, an audience of teachers may want to see how your message affects their field using emotional appeals.

2. Acknowledge and Respect Different Perspectives

Self-affirmation theory tells us that people will listen to and engage with arguments that challenge their beliefs if their core values are respected. It suggests that when you take the extra step to ensure people feel secure in their identity and values, they are less likely to perceive your ideas as an attack on their systems. This is useful if you're in a situation that requires negotiations or if you want to alter opinions or behaviors—acknowledging your audience's viewpoint without prompting increases the chances that they will trust your opinions and creates the space for meaningful discourse.

3. Balance Emotion and Logic

We discussed this in Law 21, but as an added note, emotional appeal and logical reasoning are central to persuasion. Studies in dual-process theories of persuasion, such as the Elaboration Likelihood Model, demonstrate that audiences process messages through two routes: the central (logic-driven) and the peripheral (emotion-driven). Messages that engage both pathways are more likely to be persuasive and memorable.

As an effective communicator, you must actively engage with your audience's reactions and be flexible when adapting your messages. Allow for edits and touch-ups because you cannot plan for everyone in your audience in the same way; you cannot completely control what the weather will be like. Watching for cues like body language, verbal feedback, or engagement levels can help you determine which parts of your message are being received better than others. You must be adaptable to understand the feedback and appropriately adjust your tone, pace, or content to ensure maximum engagement.

CONCLUSION

Throughout this book, we have embarked on a journey to help us understand not just how to influence others but also the power of that influence and how it works. Human psychology is multifaceted, and we have explored 21 timeless laws of psychology that demonstrate this complexity. We have viewed our interactions with others through the lens of psychology and noticed how much influence we exert on the people in our lives. At the core of it, influence is about connection and the human desire to belong and succeed.

As we wrap up this book, consider each law we have explored. I'll leave you with homework. Imagine meeting a stranger at a coffee shop, someone you think will make a good partner or friend. I'll extend it further and say it might even be someone you believe will be an excellent match for your business as a client. How will you apply each of these laws to influence and connect with them subtly? If you can create a step-by-step guide for navigating that situation, then I know I have done my job and that you have successfully understood these laws of psychology.

Printed in Dunstable, United Kingdom

65863661R00087